Overflow: Living Above Life's Limits

Overflow: Living Above Life's Limits

Kenneth Hagin Jr.

First Printing 2006
ISBN–13: 978-0-89276-745-8
ISBN–10: 0-89276-745-6

In the U.S. write:
Kenneth Hagin Ministries
P.O. Box 50126
Tulsa, OK 74150-0126
1-888-28-FAITH
www.rhema.org

In Canada write:
Kenneth Hagin Ministries
P.O. Box 335, Station D
Etobicoke (Toronto), Ontario
Canada, M9A 4X3
www.rhemacanada.org

"... I came that they may have and enjoy life,
and have it in abundance ... till it *overflows*."
                                        —John 10:10 (*Amplified*)

contents

part one

Personal Requirements for Living in the Overflow

c h a p t e r *1*

Overflow Blessings—God Wants You to Have Them!

Picture yourself standing near the top of one of the largest waterfalls in the world. The rushing water thunders so loudly that you can barely hear the sound of your own voice. The spray kicks up so high and carries so far that even hundreds of feet away, you still get drenched to the bone. Can you imagine what an intense, awe-inspiring experience that would be?

That's exactly where I found myself as I stood gazing in awe at the majestic Victoria Falls, situated on the Zambezi River bordering Zimbabwe and Zambia, Africa. My wife, Lynette, and I visited Victoria Falls on our way from a crusade in Zambia to meetings in Botswana. Known as one of the seven wonders of the modern world, these falls are approximately one mile wide. The mist from the falls is so thick, it's like being in a soaking rainstorm. I've never seen anything like it.

We visited the area in March, the wet season, when the water cascades over Victoria Falls in a vast, unbroken expanse. It's the time of year when visitors see the *maximum* flow of water, and it is an amazing sight! I couldn't help but think, *I've never seen so much water in my entire life!*

As I stood amazed at the mighty abundance of water flowing over those cliffs, I had a revelation: God wants you and me to experience the same kind of overflowing abundance in our lives that I was witnessing in nature at Victoria Falls!

You and I can have the *maximum flow* of God's blessings. We can enjoy *fullness of life* greater than we have ever imagined! God desires life in abundance for every one of His children. It's the very reason Jesus came to earth! God left no one out in the great plan of redemption that Jesus consummated 2,000 years ago, making it possible for *anyone* to walk in God's overflowing blessings.

In the following pages, we're going to explore this great truth in detail, beginning with a pivotal statement Jesus made that serves to contrast Satan's activities with Jesus' own activities in the earth.

JOHN 10:10
10 The thief comes only to steal and kill and destroy; I [Jesus] have come that they may have life, and have it to the full.

JOHN 10:10 (*KJV*)
10 The thief cometh not, but for to steal, and to kill, and to destroy: I am come that they might have life, and that they might have it more abundantly.

I especially like the way this verse reads in *The Amplified Bible*.

> **JOHN 10:10** (*Amplified*)
> **10** The thief comes only in order to steal and kill and destroy. I came that they may have and enjoy life, and have it in abundance (to the full, till it overflows).

Let's focus for a moment on the last phrase in John 10:10 from *The Amplified Bible*: "I came that they may have and enjoy life, and have it in abundance (to the full, till it overflows)." What does it mean to enjoy life in abundance—to the full, till it overflows? I will not only endeavor to explain that in the pages of this book; I will show you how to live the abundant life for yourself—how to make living above the limits of life a reality for you.

The abundant life that Jesus came to give us is not a vague sort of blessing that can't be explained. And yet, most people can't tell you exactly what it means to live in this blessing of "life more abundantly" that Jesus promised in John 10:10.

For example, if I were to ask, "What is the biggest thing you think God can do?" most Christians would probably answer, "Oh, there's no limit to what God can do!"

And if I were to ask, "What is the biggest thing you think God can do for *you*?" many Christians would answer, "No matter what happens in my life, God can take care of it."

Then if I were to ask, "What is the biggest thing you think God can do for you *today*?" many would generally respond, "Well, whatever I need."

But none of these answers properly explains what it means to have "life more abundantly," or to live in the overflow blessings of God.

In studying this subject of overflow, I want us to get down to real living—to brass tacks or to where the rubber meets the road, as some would say. There are too many sincere, well-meaning Christians struggling today in poverty and lack. They feel the restrictions and limitations of life pressing in upon them. They're not seeing that God intends to bless them with a "Victoria Falls" kind of abundance. They're not living life to the full, till it overflows.

Some have even begun to deny the reality of God's abundance. But the truth is, God delights in our prosperity (Ps. 35:27). It is His good pleasure to give us the kingdom (Luke 12:32)! It is just as Jesus said: "I came that they may have and enjoy life, and have it in abundance (to the full, till it overflows)" (John 10:10 *Amplified*)!

God's Word: The Ultimate Authority on God's Will

The Word of God is the supreme valid authority in determining what God really desires for His children. In other words, it doesn't matter what you think, what you've been taught, or what others say about it. The only thing that matters is, what does *God* say? What does God's Word have to say about His will for our lives?

You see, everyone has his or her idea of what abundance is. But let's look to the Bible and see what *God* has to say about it. Until you realize that it is God's will for you to live in abundant overflow, you will not progress to living above life's limits. I have selected just a few verses that deal directly or indirectly with abundance. But I also encourage you to search the Scriptures for yourself, as there are many more verses that prove the fact that God wants His people blessed!

> **PSALM 23:1** (*KJV*)
> 1 The Lord is my shepherd; I shall not want.

The *New International Version* reads, "The Lord is my shepherd, I shall not be in want."

> **PSALM 37:3–4**
> 3 Trust in the Lord and do good; dwell in the land and enjoy safe pasture.
> 4 Delight yourself in the Lord and he will give you the desires of your heart.

> **MATTHEW 6:33**
> 33 But seek first his kingdom and his righteousness, and all these things will be given to you as well.

> **MARK 11:24**
> 24 Therefore I [Jesus] tell you, whatever you ask for in prayer, believe that you have received it, and it will be yours.

Let's focus on this last verse, Mark 11:24, for a moment, especially the phrase "whatever you ask for in prayer." Some will say, "Oh, that just means *spiritual* things; you can believe God only for *those* kinds of things."

But notice there is no such qualification in this verse. It says, *"Whatever* you ask for in prayer . . . ."* That means that whatever you find in God's Word that He has promised or has provided for you, you can believe Him for it! *Whatever!*

Well, if you're enjoying "whatever you ask for in prayer," you're walking in abundance! You're living in the overflow blessings of God!

3 JOHN 2 (*NKJV*)
2 Beloved, I pray that you may prosper in all things and be in health, just as your soul prospers.

In this verse, John said, "I pray that you may prosper in *all* things." That's not just talking about spiritual things. God is saying He wants His people to prosper (materially or financially) and be in health (referring to our physical bodies) even as our soul prospers (talking about our mind, will, and emotions).

Let's continue reading a few more New Testament verses that describe the abundance that God desires for you.

2 CORINTHIANS 8:9
9 For you know the grace of our Lord Jesus Christ, that though he was rich, yet for your sakes he became poor, so that you through his poverty might become rich.

Jesus came to this world and took upon Himself the poverty *we* should have had, so that we could experience what *He* had before He came here to earth. One dictionary definition of the word *rich* is "having a full supply." Well, what did He have? Do you think

He lacked anything? No, He had abundance! He took our nothingness so that through Him, we could have abundance—life to the full, till it overflows!

> **PHILIPPIANS 4:19**
> **19** And my God will meet all your needs according to his glorious riches in Christ Jesus.

This verse says God will meet all of your needs, but it also implies abundance. In other words, you don't have to look just to *your* ability and resources. He said that He would meet your needs according to *His* riches in glory!

Does God have any riches in glory? *He does!* Did Jesus pay the price for you to obtain God's blessings and walk in them in abundance? *He did!* Obviously, God wants *you* to live in abundance, in fullness—until you overflow life's limits!

Preparing for Overflow

We've looked at God's Word—His will—concerning abundance and overflow. If we are going to experience the abundant overflow that enables us to overcome life's limitations, then we must lay the foundation of His Word in our lives. In other words, we must become convinced that God wants us to have this abundance.

After we've laid the proper foundation concerning God's Word, we must do something to prepare *ourselves* to enter into God's abundance.

You will never walk in God's abundance and live in the overflow above life's limitations unless you're prepared to do it. Let me illustrate this truth. If you have a driver's license, do you remember the day you got that license? The promise of driving *yourself* around rather than being limited to depending on others lay just ahead. That was a great day, wasn't it? But on the day you became old enough to get a driver's license, you didn't march down to the office where they were processing applications and just get the license. No, you had to do a few things first. For example, you had to prepare to take a written test. Then you had to prepare to take a driving test.

I remember when my son, Craig, became old enough to get a driver's license. He began preparing himself to pass the parallel parking portion of the driving test. We practiced parallel parking over and over again so that when the time came for him to take the test, he could do it. He passed the test with flying colors!

Similarly, for us to walk in and enjoy the overflow blessings of God, some preparation has to take place. And that preparation takes place in the mind. You have to prepare your mind by training it to think in line with God's Word. You have to prepare your mind to think God's thoughts continually. How do you do that? By renewing your mind with the Word—by reading, studying, and meditating on what God has to say about you.

In addition, to prepare yourself for overflow, you must understand God's priorities, and make *His* priorities *your* priorities.

Putting First Things First:
A Vision for the Lost

To live in the overflow, you must know and understand that abundance is what God wants for you. But you must also realize that you can't get so wrapped up in the pursuit of abundance that you forget about doing the work God wants you to do. What does God want us to do?

First, He wants us to fulfill the Great Commission (Mark 16:15–18). He wants us to focus on getting people saved in our sphere of influence—our neighborhoods, our workplaces, our towns and cities, and so forth—as well as in the uttermost parts of the world. Unfortunately, it seems that many people are preaching prosperity, and few are talking about getting the lost saved.

As we've seen from the Scriptures, there is no question that God wants us to have prosperity and live in the overflow above life's limitations. But while we're enjoying all that abundance, we *must* maintain our vision for the lost! That's why Jesus came in the first place: to seek and save the lost (Luke 19:10)—to provide salvation and redemption for them. Thank God for that "so great salvation" (Heb. 2:3 *KJV*) which includes threefold redemption benefits: redemption from spiritual death, from sickness and disease, and from poverty. But at the same time, we must maintain our priorities.

Sadly, many Christians focus on those benefits and forget the job they were given to do. For example, do you work for an employer? Are benefits included at your place of employment? In addition to the salary they offer, many companies and organizations provide benefits, such as retirement, health insurance, and paid vacation time.

But what would happen if you became more concerned about your benefits than you were about doing your actual job? You wouldn't last very long, and as a result, you would no longer enjoy those benefits!

Similarly, we must be about the business of what God has commissioned us to do. As we trust and obey Him and His Word, those benefits—the life more abundantly that Jesus provided—are ours to receive and enjoy!

At this point, when you begin talking about obeying and serving God, it seems that some people want to get into the ditch of a "works" mentality about receiving the blessings of God. They forget that God has given us all things to enjoy (1 Tim. 6:17). The Bible also says in Romans 8:32 that *"He who did not spare his own Son, but gave him up for us all—how will he not also, along with him, graciously give us all things?"*

We must have the attitude that because God loves us so much, we will love Him too. We will trust and obey Him implicitly with all of our heart, mind, body, and strength (Matt. 22:37; Mark 12:30; Luke 10:27).

God loved us so much that He sent His Son to die for us so that we could have life more abundantly—to the full, till it overflows. Why wouldn't we, in turn, wholeheartedly obey Someone Who has done all of that for us and Who would do anything for us that we asked? Therefore, our wholehearted obedience to God and His Word is the key to preparing to receive and walk in God's overflow blessings.

An Attitude for Overflow

Our main text says, "The thief comes only in order to steal and kill and destroy. I came that they may have and enjoy life, and have it in abundance (to the full, till it overflows)" (John 10:10 *Amplified*). We have established that Jesus came to give us abundant life. But how do we receive that life so we are enjoying it—so we are actually *living* it?

One of the first things we must do to live this abundant, over-flowing life is adopt an attitude for overflow.

Have you ever heard the saying, "Your attitude determines your altitude"? That saying has been trivialized over the years, but its message is ever true. The attitudes you embrace in life will determine the level of your success and well-being.

Ephesians 4:23 says, *"Be made new in the attitude of your minds."* Some people must take on a new attitude if they are going to live in the overflow as God intends. You probably know people who have the mentality that "the glass is half empty" versus "the glass is half full." Those people have a negative attitude. It seems they are always complaining about what's not right, what they don't have, and so forth.

On the other side of the coin are those who see the glass as half full. These people are thankful for what they have—for their half-full glass—and are expecting God to fill it up!

Similarly, we can go through life focusing on what we don't have, or we can focus on the blessings we do have and on the possibilities that await us.

You know, two people can hear the same sermon, and one can come away from that message with a can-do attitude, while the other continues to talk about the impossibilities and what he *can't* do. What makes the difference? One person is willing to line up his thinking and believing with the Word of God. The other person is siding with his thoughts, feelings, past experiences, or present circumstances. He is agreeing with the imposing limitations arrayed against him. The Word does not hold the place of prominence in that person's thinking that it should.

So you can see how two people facing the same type of circumstances can display different attitudes. One person can have a defeated attitude and end up a victim of circumstances. The other person can have a conqueror's attitude and end up overcoming the circumstances and limitations of life.

What is *attitude*? Your attitude is your outlook, or the way you look at life. You can have an attitude for overflow and expect more out of life. Or you can have a "half-empty" attitude that dwells on and talks about everything that has gone wrong and that will probably go wrong in the future. Really, the latter is an attitude of unbelief. Why? Because instead of measuring your beliefs by the Word of God, you measure them by your experiences in life—by what you can feel and see. And often these experiences will limit you, if you let them.

I'm talking about attitude from a spiritual standpoint. Even in the natural, however, a person's attitude affects the level of success he or she enjoys. Studies have shown that 85 percent of the reason people land good jobs and get ahead on those jobs is their attitude, while only 15 percent of the reason is the specific skills the applicant holds.

Our attitude will affect everything around us—our job, our home, our relationships, and our achievements. I'm not saying that negative things never happen to positive people. Negative things happen to everyone at one time or another. But positive people react differently to negative circumstances, and their positive attitude positively affects their eventual outcome.

Problems will come to all of us at some time or another. Everyone faces tests and trials in life. But our attitude will either enable us to bounce back or keep us bound in defeat.

Some people say, "Well, I've always been a little negative. I come from a long line of pessimists. This is just the way I am."

But did you know that no matter who you are or what happened in your past, you can *choose* the kind of attitude you will have in life?

"That sounds too simplistic," someone said. But you do have a choice. And I'll let you in on a little secret: The words you speak have more to do with your choices than you may realize. In other words, in the face of adversity, you can make a choice to overcome by saying, for example, "I refuse to let this get to me. I refuse to let this situation affect my attitude. I refuse to allow this problem to limit me. This is the day the Lord hath made; I *will* rejoice and be glad in it" (Ps. 118:24).

My dad, Kenneth E. Hagin, used to tell me, "Son, it's your choice whether you're going to be positive or negative. But I will tell you this: If you will stay positive, things will always get better and go well. But if you stay negative, things will not go well for you."

Much of what my father said to me had to do with outlook, or attitude. In this chapter, I'm going to share with you several godly attitudes that will position you to live above life's circumstances, in the abundant overflow that God wants you to experience.

Attitude: 'God Is for Me!'

If you want to live in the overflow, one attitude you must develop is a *God-is-for-me* attitude!

ROMANS 8:31
31 . . . If God is for us, who can be against us?

The Apostle Paul had the attitude that God was for him—God was on his side—no matter what. No matter what happened, no matter what the circumstance, Paul knew that God was still there with him and that God was *for* him!

Some people have the attitude that everyone's against them. Because of life's experiences, they have adopted a *poor-me* attitude.

They think the whole world is against them and that no one is willing to help them. Sadly, many of those people navigate through their entire lives with that mentality, and their wrong beliefs cause them to miss the many blessings God has for them.

We must look to the Word of God and realize once and for all that God is on our side and that He is always working on our behalf if we'll trust Him! We may not always see it, but God and His Word cannot lie. If He said He'd never leave us, then He will never leave us! If He said He's for us, then He's for us! We need never face our tests and trials alone. God is with us, and He's *for* us! He is an ever-present help in the time of trouble (Ps. 46:1)!

Some people will accept the fact that God is for them in times of trouble as long as the trouble is not something they brought upon themselves. But what about the times when we are responsible for the trouble in our lives? There are times when things go wrong because we've done something to cause trouble to come. Yes, we have to take responsibility for it and say, "Yes, this is all my fault, and I am sorry." But then we can also say with confidence, "Yet, my God is still for me. He has not left me; He has not forsaken me. God is for me, not against me. He is on my side!"

If we have sinned or missed it in some way, we need to take responsibility for that. We need to ask God to forgive us and, perhaps, ask others to forgive us. But we must never forget the fact that God loves us and is for us.

You see, God decided a long time ago that He was going to be for you. He had already made His decision when Adam and Eve fell and plunged into a state of sin that caused them to be banished from the Presence of God. Before the foundation of the world, God had planned to send His Son, Jesus, to earth to die on the

Cross for the sins of mankind. When God raised Jesus from the dead, as far as God was concerned, He raised us with Him so that all who believe in Jesus and call upon His Name would be saved from eternal death and be brought into right-standing with God, the Father.

God has always wanted a relationship with man, His creation. When Adam committed high treason in the Garden of Eden by disobeying God, God was still on Adam's side! It was as if God was saying, "I am for the man I created. Even though Satan has robbed him and has stolen him away, I am still for him; and I have a plan!" And through God's great plan of redemption, He purchased us back from the enemy; He bought our freedom. We can have a relationship with Him today through Jesus' death, burial, and resurrection.

I remember when a member of our church congregation who was in the military was about to be deployed to the Middle East. Before he left, I put my arm around him and hugged him. I told him, "We are here for you, and we are praying for you." Similarly, I want you to imagine God sitting down beside you, slipping His arm around you, and saying, "I'm right here. I will not leave you. And I am for you. I'm on your side."

The very act of God sending His only Son to die for us is God's resounding commitment to us: "I am *for* you!" And God will never change His mind about us. Malachi 3:6 says, "For I am the Lord, I change not" (*KJV*). What He said when He sent Jesus to us, He is still saying today: "You belong to Me, and I am *for* you!"

Take hold of that attitude! No matter what the devil has tried to do to you, you can boldly proclaim, "God is for me! Who can be against me? No weapon formed against me will prosper because God is *for* me" (Rom. 8:31; Isa. 54:17).

Attitude: 'God Is Generous Toward Me!'

If you want to live in the overflow, another attitude you must develop is a *God-is-generous-toward-me* attitude!

> **MATTHEW 7:11**
> 11 If you, then, though you are evil [or natural], know how to give good gifts to your children, how much more will your Father in heaven give good gifts to those who ask him!

This verse really says it all: If we, being natural, know how to bless our children, *how much more* does God, our Heavenly Father, know how to bless us as His children? We need to develop that *how-much-more* mentality in receiving from God and His Word.

Let's look at Matthew 7:11 in the *King James Version* with some of the verses that precede this verse.

> **MATTHEW 7:7–11** (*KJV*)
> 7 Ask, and it shall be given you; seek, and ye shall find; knock, and it shall be opened unto you:
> 8 For every one that asketh receiveth; and he that seeketh findeth; and to him that knocketh it shall be opened.
> 9 Or what man is there of you, whom if his son ask bread, will he give him a stone?
> 10 Or if he ask a fish, will he give him a serpent?
> 11 If ye then, being evil, know how to give good gifts unto your children, how much more shall your Father which is in heaven give good things to them that ask him?

This passage is comparing the relationship a child has with his natural father to the relationship we have with God, our Heavenly Father. Verses 7 and 8 tell us that we can expect to receive results from our prayers and petitions to God. Verses 9 through 11 show us the generosity of God.

God is a generous God! He is not stingy! And to receive from Him, we must adopt the mindset that God is a giver. We must have the attitude that, not only is God a giver, but He is also willing to pour out His generosity and abundance on *us*!

We must avoid at all costs the limiting, negative attitude that God will only give us enough to get by. We must rid ourselves of any *poor-me* attitude. You might say, "But I don't have anything. And I've *never* had much of anything. I don't expect things will ever be different." Well, with that attitude, things will *never* be different. If you want things to change for the better, you have to take hold of the attitude that God is a generous God and that He is generous toward *you*!

Although there are many scriptures we could look at that illustrate the generosity of God, I want to look at the following two verses.

PHILIPPIANS 4:19
19 And my God will meet all your needs according to his glorious riches in Christ Jesus.

JAMES 1:17
17 Every good and perfect gift is from above, coming down from the Father of the heavenly lights, who does not change like shifting shadows.

If you are born again, God is your Heavenly Father; He is going to take care of you. He will meet all your needs according to His riches in glory, not according to your own might or strength. And He will never change.

These verses show us the Person and character of God. Without the proper knowledge of God, we cannot receive from Him and walk in His overflow blessings. In other words, to *receive* from God generously—abundantly, to the full, above life's limitations—we must know Him as One Who *gives* generously.

Have you ever had a serious need and thought about going to a certain person to ask for help? But then you thought, *It's no use. He could help me, all right. But he never helps anybody; he's just not very generous.* You couldn't go to that individual with confidence, because you knew that he or she was not known for being a giver.

Similarly, when it comes to having faith and confidence in God, we must know Who it is we are dealing with! We have to see Him for Who He really is—a giver! And God is not just a giver; He is a *generous* giver!

Psalm 145:16 says about God, *"You open your hand and satisfy the desires of every living thing."* Notice the last part of that verse says, "of *every* living thing." In addition to having the attitude that God is generous, you must have the attitude that what He has done for anyone else, He will also do for you!

God does not have any favorites (Acts 10:34). As far as God is concerned, we are all His favorites. Therefore, you could say about yourself with confidence, "*I* am God's favorite!"

When a parent, grandparent, aunt, or uncle is acting fairly, all the children in that person's life—sons and daughters, grandsons and granddaughters, and nephews and nieces—feel as though they are that person's favorite. But many times people have a natural preference toward one child over another. But if we're fair about it, we will treat each child the same.

Your Heavenly Father treats His children the same too. He is no respecter of persons. Some may be blessed more than others because of certain choices they've made in life. As my father always said, "We need to find out how God works and work with Him." Yet, so many people never grasp this truth. They want God to bless them on their own terms—regardless of the choices they make in life—and then they wonder why things don't go well for them.

Sadly, those people don't realize that although they are just as qualified for the blessings of God as the next person, they need to adopt and develop the right attitudes and beliefs about God. They need to renew their mind with His Word until they think like He thinks—until they see things as He sees them. Then, and only then, will their life bear fruit and take on new meaning.

What are you expecting from God today? Some people aren't expecting very much, and that is all they will receive in life: *not very much*! They are born again but have never lifted their sights to see all the possibilities that exist for them in God. Their attitude is, *I'm just thankful to be saved. I'm not going to push it any further than that. God saved me and that's all I really need.*

Friend, did you know that in Christ, you have been automatically qualified to receive every blessing God has provided in His plan of redemption? Colossians 1:12 says that the Father *"has qualified you to share in the inheritance of the saints in the kingdom of light."* God has qualified you! If you have been born again by the blood of the Lord Jesus Christ, you qualify for *every* blessing He has promised in His Word.

It would help you to say out loud: "I qualify for all the generous promises of God. They belong to me, and He will not withhold from me. I am His favorite child!"

Attitude: 'With God, All Things Are Possible for Me!'

A third attitude we must have if we want to live in the overflow is the *with-God-all-things-are-possible* attitude.

> **LUKE 18:27**
> 27 . . . "What is impossible with men is possible with God."

That verse happens to be one of my favorites, because it speaks of the limitlessness of God. Meditating on and believing this verse will take the limits off your life too. The things you thought you couldn't do before will become possibilities in Him. The things you thought you couldn't accomplish suddenly are within reach.

In this country, we have speed limits posted on our roads and highways that limit how fast we travel on these roadways. But I have been to Germany and have ridden on the Autobahn, where there are no speed limits! And some people there drive on the Autobahn as fast as their vehicle will allow them to go! I have ridden in a car on the Autobahn going 170 miles per hour! We could do that because on that particular roadway, there were no limits as to how fast you can go. (You'd just better have both hands on the wheel and be alert, because you cover a lot of ground in a hurry!)

Similarly, with God, we can cover a lot of ground in just a little bit of time, because with Him, all things are possible. There are no limits with God. He is the Limitless One! And we need to develop the attitude that says, *There is no limit to what God can and will do for me. And He is doing it for me now!*

Have you ever been in a situation in which you presented an idea and somebody else piped up and said, "That will never work; it's impossible"? Have you ever discovered that some of those ideas you had were *not* impossible?

Sometimes, the only thing separating you from limitless possibilities in God is your attitude. There will always be those in life who will try to throw water on your fire! But you don't have to let them do it. You may have nothing left of your God-given dream but a few embers and a little smoke. But you can take the Word of God in your heart and mouth and, with the right attitude, rise to victory! You can fan those embers until the fire of God's Word burns brightly and deeply in your heart once again. And you can expect to see those dreams come true, because *with God, all things are possible*!

Sometimes it may look as if we're living in anything but the abundant life. The tests and trials of life come to all of us to try and shake our faith in the possibilities of God. But I like what one author said: "When my attitudes are right, there's no barrier too high, no valley too deep, no dream too extreme, no challenge too great for me."[1]

If you're going to make it through tough times in life, you must have a tough attitude—an attitude that believes God, no matter what the situation or how the circumstances appear. And you're going to have to be *determined* to believe with everything that's in you that all things are possible with God!

You know, a winning athlete doesn't excel at what he does just by watching a film, reading a manual, or listening to a lecture by the coach. No, he has to *condition* himself to win. And he does that, not by just conditioning his body, but by conditioning his *attitude*. He prepares himself physically and then he develops the determined attitude that he *will* win—he *will* overcome!

The difference between a good athlete and a great athlete is the level of determination each applies to playing the game. You can see why your attitude has so much to do with the success you enjoy in life. One of my favorite sayings is, "I cannot be defeated, and I will not quit!" That's the attitude we have to develop and maintain if we're going to live in the overflow blessings of God.

---

[1] Charles R. Swindoll, *Strengthening Your Grip: Essentials in an Aimless World* (Waco, TX: Word Books, 1982), 207.

Giants and Grasshoppers in the Valley of Decision—Will You *Conquer* or *Quit?*

Let's read our text scripture, John 10:10, once again from *The Amplified Bible*: "The thief comes only in order to steal and kill and destroy. I came that they may have and enjoy life, and have it in abundance (to the full, till it overflows)."

That life in abundance—to the full, till it overflows—speaks of God's highest and best, doesn't it? This is what God intends for every one of His children. Yet, so many aren't enjoying this kind of overflowing life.

What keeps people from enjoying the best that God has for their lives? Why do some never reach the level of life that God has promised in His Word? I believe one reason is their mentality toward the obstacles—the situations and circumstances—in life that confront them. In other words, they will believe God's Word until a circumstance arises that contradicts the Word. Then they have more faith in the circumstance than in the Word of God.

I read a survey once that said 95 percent of people live according to what their body or their fleshly desires tell them. Their whole life consists of living from one fleshly desire to another. Only about 5 percent live according to what they believe. And about 8 out of 10 in that group think and believe what others tell them to think and believe!

Only a very small percentage of the people in that particular survey truly think and believe in line with God and His Word and with what He has said about their lives and their futures. Now, I don't know the level of accuracy of this particular survey. But if it is even close to being correct, it is an astounding statement about the mental attitude of people.

Our beliefs—what we believe in our heart—should determine our attitude, our mindset or mentality. And if we are believing the Word of God, we should have a positive mental attitude. One of the greatest privileges you and I have as believers is that we can take the Word of God and develop the mentality that God wants us to have, one that will position us to receive and walk in His abundance and overflow!

Your thinking will affect your believing and your speaking—what you're saying—about your life. So you absolutely must learn to think right before you'll ever be able to experience the things that God has made available to you.

I want to show you some truths in this area from the example of the people of Israel in the Old Testament. The Apostle Paul said,

"These things happened to them as EXAMPLES and were written down as warnings for us, on whom the fulfilment of the ages has come" (1 Cor. 10:11). Let's look at how God's people responded to His promise of abundance and to the opportunity to live in the overflow that He had provided for them.

After the children of Israel exited Egypt, a land of slavery, God's intention was to bring them into their Promised Land, a land of plenty—a land of overflow! Then Moses sent 12 spies into the land to look it over and report their findings back to Moses and the people.

> **NUMBERS 13:17–20**
> **17** When Moses sent them to explore Canaan, he said, "Go up through the Negev and on into the hill country.
> **18** See what the land is like and whether the people who live there are strong or weak, few or many.
> **19** What kind of land do they live in? Is it good or bad? What kind of towns do they live in? Are they unwalled or fortified?
> **20** How is the soil? Is it fertile or poor? Are there trees on it or not? Do your best to bring back some of the fruit of the land." (It was the season for the first ripe grapes.)

We know from reading the entire account that these spies went into the land and remained there for 40 days. According to verse 23 of this passage, they cut down a branch containing a cluster of grapes; it was so big that they had to put it on a pole for two men to carry! The Promised Land was truly a land of abundance!

Now let's look at the report these men brought back to Moses and the people.

> NUMBERS 13:27–29,31–33 (*KJV*)
> 27 . . . We came unto the land whither thou sentest us, and surely it floweth with milk and honey; and this is the fruit of it.
> 28 *Nevertheless* the people be strong that dwell in the land, and the cities are walled, and very great: and moreover we saw the children of Anak there.
> 29 The Amalekites dwell in the land of the south: and the Hittites, and the Jebusites, and the Amorites, dwell in the mountains: and the Canaanites dwell by the sea, and by the coast of Jordan. . . .
> 31 But the men that went up with him said, We be not able to go up against the people; for they are stronger than we.
> 32 And they brought up an evil report of the land which they had searched unto the children of Israel, saying, The land, through which we have gone to search it, is a land that eateth up the inhabitants thereof; and all the people that we saw in it are men of a great stature.
> 33 And there we saw the giants, the sons of Anak, which come of the giants: and we were in our own sight as grasshoppers, and so we were in their sight.

All the spies agreed that the land was a land of overflow just as God had said. But notice verse 28. After they reported all the good things they had seen there, they said, "*Nevertheless* the people be strong that dwell in the land, and the cities are walled, and very great: and moreover we saw the children of Anak there (*KJV*)."

Ten of the spies then proceeded to tell why they couldn't enter into and possess that which God had promised them.

Look at verse 33 in the *New International Version*, "... We seemed like grasshoppers in our own eyes, and we looked the same to them."

Have you ever heard the phrase "grasshopper mentality"? Ten of the twelve spies Moses sent to spy out the Promised Land had this attitude toward God's promises. I have heard "grasshopper mentality" defined as *an inner disease that seldom is diagnosed but is deadly to the person's future.* It's true. A person with a grasshopper mentality thinks, *I'm so much smaller than the opposition, I'm not able to overcome. I am a nobody, a loser.* And because he thinks that way, he eventually believes it, and all his words and actions reflect his mentality.

No believer should ever have a grasshopper mentality! Yet, so many have developed this very attitude. They think they can't win in life. They think they are limited. They believe that the odds are stacked against them so that they just can't overcome. The life they settle for reflects what they think is possible.

You probably know of people today with the mentality of those 10 unbelieving spies. They read the Bible, but they really don't believe what it says. They won't act on what they read. Some of these same people will holler "Amen" to a good message at church, but nothing changes for them in life. They have numerous reasons why the Word won't work for them and why things will never get better. These Christians with a grasshopper mentality might shout to the Lord in church, yet they shake in terror when the problems of life appear on the horizon.

These people, like the 10 spies we read about in Numbers chapter 13, have a defeatist attitude in life. When obstacles and challenges arise, they are defeated in their own mind, and they fail before they even begin to fight!

I want you to notice that those 10 spies in Numbers chapter 13 felt inferior and then acted on what they believed. They were moved by what they felt more than by what God had said. They said, in essence, "We feel like grasshoppers compared to those giants. And that's the way the giants see us too!"

Now, they never talked to those giants. How could they know what the giants were thinking? They didn't *know* that's how the giants saw them. But they became overwhelmed by their own negative thoughts. Their wrong thinking produced wrong believing, and their wrong beliefs produced the wrong kind of action.

A person with a grasshopper mentality focuses on his weaknesses instead of on his strengths. But it doesn't matter how weak you feel—God is your strength! God's Word and His Spirit will put you over if you will dare to take hold of the greatness of God in your thought life instead of your own weaknesses, shortcomings, faults, and failures.

Don't focus on your weaknesses! Instead, focus on the Word of God and on what *God* has said you can do. The Apostle Paul wrote in Philippians 4:13, "I can do all things through Christ which strengtheneth me" (*KJV*). Jesus said that all things are possible to him who believes (Mark 9:23)!

So many believers see themselves as weak and unworthy. They go through life looking for a day of relief! But what you think about yourself will eventually become what you believe about yourself. And you will ultimately become what you believe.

Some believers today develop a grasshopper mentality in life. They're saved, all right, but they have let circumstances beat them down and limit them. Others develop a conqueror's mentality. They go out armed with the Word of God and possess His promises!

The attitude of the 10 spies was, *We can't!* And because of their attitude, *they couldn't!* They were looking at all the circumstances instead of looking at God and His Word. They went from being people of promise, to whom God had promised great abundance, to people without hope who would wander through life in the wilderness with no goals or dreams for a better tomorrow. Their grasshopper mentality caused them to live a very small and limited existence.

Some people are always trying to hide from tests and trials. But as I said previously, the tests and trials of life come to all of us. We are never going to get away from that fact until Jesus comes back, because right now, the devil is the god of this world (2 Cor. 4:4). And he has come to steal, kill, and destroy (John 10:10).

We might as well take hold of the strength of God and, by the power of His Word and His Spirit, face the giants that are trying to stand in the way of what God has for us. What have we got to lose? If we run and hide, we are going to go through life blessed only to a measure, with vague memories of unfulfilled dreams. But if we stand our ground and fight the good fight of faith (1 Tim. 6:12), we have everything to gain! I don't know about you, but I want to trust God and live in the overflow!

Are You 'the Ten' or 'the Two'?

Of the 12 spies whom Moses sent into Canaan, the Promised Land, two came back with the right mindset or attitude. Caleb and Joshua didn't have a grasshopper mentality; they had a conqueror's mentality. They had the attitude that if God said it, they were well able to do it and that if God gave it, they were well able to possess it!

Numbers 13:30 says, "And Caleb stilled [or silenced] the people before Moses, and said, Let us go up at once, and possess it; for we are well able to overcome it" (*KJV*). First, I want you to notice that Caleb had to "still" the people. Why did he have to do that? Because they had listened to the negative, unbelieving report of the 10 spies, and fear had no doubt gripped their hearts. Those people were probably caught up in a frenzy after hearing about all the giants and the great, fortified cities they were going to have to face if they obeyed God.

Let's look at something else in Numbers chapter 14 that Joshua and Caleb said to the people that showed the mentality of these two men of God.

NUMBERS 14:6–9
6 Joshua son of Nun and Caleb son of Jephunneh, who were among those who had explored the land, tore their clothes
7 and said to the entire Israelite assembly, "The land we passed through and explored is exceedingly good.
8 If the Lord is pleased with us, he will lead us into that land, a land flowing with milk and honey, and will give it to us.

9 Only do not rebel against the Lord. And do not be afraid of the people of the land, because we will swallow them up. Their protection is gone, but the Lord is with us. Do not be afraid of them."

I want you to notice in verses 8 and 9 that Joshua and Caleb had a conqueror's mentality based on God and on what He had said, not based on themselves. God had promised them the land, and they trusted Him. They had seen God perform wonders from their deliverance from Egypt to their encampment at Kadesh, where they now stood on the brink of entering the Promised Land. So their mentality was in no way based on mind over matter. It was based on God Himself!

In the *King James Version*, the last part of verse 9 says, "Their defence is departed from them." Joshua was talking about their enemies. In other words, Joshua was saying, "They are up against God now—they don't stand a chance!"

In our own lives today, when we look at our problems, we need to see them in the light of *God's* power and ability, not our human limitations. We know that those circumstances are no match for Him. Their defense has departed from them! Those circumstances don't have a chance against God—and since God is for you, they don't have a chance against *you*!

Joshua and Caleb: A Conqueror's Mentality

Let's look more closely at the things that stand out about Joshua and Caleb. First, they were not intimidated by their enemies. They were not moved by their circumstances. Instead, they focused on the greatness of God. They focused on what they would be enjoying once they entered the land God had given them.

Similarly, our attitude today must be based on God and what He has said, not on what we can see. Second Corinthians 4:18 says, *"So we fix our eyes not on what is seen, but on what is unseen. For what is seen is temporary, but what is unseen is eternal."* The Apostle Paul was saying here that the things that are seen are temporary; they are subject to change. But the *unseen* things, or the things God has promised us that we must believe by faith, are *eternal*; they are *not* subject to change! Hallelujah!

People with a conqueror's mentality believe, like Joshua and Caleb, that they have a destiny planned by God and that they can fulfill that destiny. Fixing their eyes on the unseen, they believe that God is greater than any giant they will ever face. And they believe that God will show Himself strong on their behalf to cause them to overcome every test, trial, or obstacle that stands in their way.

What else stands out about Joshua and Caleb? What else set them apart from those 10 unbelieving spies? Well, Joshua and Caleb possessed the promise! Their dreams were fulfilled, and they entered into that which God had planned for them—the overflow blessings of God!

Did all of this happen because Caleb and Joshua were better than the rest? No, it was because of their attitude or mindset. What they believed *about God* set them apart from the others and brought them great blessing in life. They honored and esteemed the Word of God spoken to them, and God honored them as a result. In fact, God said about Caleb in Numbers 14:24, *"Because my servant Caleb has a different spirit and follows me wholeheartedly, I will bring him into the land he went to, and his descendants will inherit it."*

God said Caleb had a different spirit than the 10 unbelieving spies who caused the people to grumble and complain against Moses and Aaron and against God. In fact, the Bible calls their grumbling against the Word of the Lord *rebellion* (Num. 14:9). But God said that Caleb had followed him fully, or wholeheartedly.

Let's read again the passage in Numbers chapter 14 that shows us what Joshua and Caleb did after the people began murmuring.

> **NUMBERS 14:5–10**
> 5 Then Moses and Aaron fell facedown in front of the whole Israelite assembly gathered there.
> 6 Joshua son of Nun and Caleb son of Jephunneh, who were among those who had explored the land, tore their clothes
> 7 and said to the entire Israelite assembly, "The land we passed through and explored is exceedingly good.
> 8 If the Lord is pleased with us, he will lead us into that land, a land flowing with milk and honey, and will give it to us.
> 9 Only do not rebel against the Lord. And do not be afraid of the people of the land, because we will swallow them up. Their protection is gone, but the Lord is with us. Do not be afraid of them."
> 10 But the whole assembly talked about stoning them. Then the glory of the Lord appeared at the Tent of Meeting to all the Israelites.

In verse 10, it says the people were going to rise up and stone Joshua and Caleb for their words. But then God intervened and protected them. It says, *"Then the glory of the Lord appeared at the Tent of Meeting to all the Israelites."* Friend, when you develop that conqueror's mentality like Joshua and Caleb, there will be those who will come against you too. But God will intervene and show Himself strong on your behalf when you are trusting in Him and His Word. When you are full of the purpose and promise of God like Joshua and Caleb were, you cannot be destroyed!

Because Joshua and Caleb followed God wholeheartedly and didn't rebel against His promise, they both entered into the Promised Land. In fact, Joshua, in Moses' stead, went on to become the leader of the people who entered the land. And we know that God wrought a tremendous victory for them at the battle of Jericho. The enemy was defeated so God's people could enter into the abundance that God had promised.

Now, when Joshua and the new generation of Israelites approached Jericho, the circumstances hadn't changed. Jericho was still a great walled city with the greatest fortifications known to man. The walls of that city were so wide that chariots could ride on them. No one in history had ever taken Jericho. But history was about to change.

Joshua and the Israelites could have taken the same grasshopper mentality as their fathers. They could have whined and moaned, "Oh, no. What are we going to do?" But they didn't! Instead, Joshua said, "Listen, guys, here's what we're going to do—we're going to conquer this city!" And he gave them the instructions God had given him for taking the city (see Joshua chapter 6).

After they entered the land, Caleb, who was then 85 years old, still had that conqueror's mentality. The following verses show us Caleb's unwavering attitude toward the promises of God.

JOSHUA 14:9–14 (*KJV*)

9 And Moses sware on that day, saying, Surely the land whereon thy [Caleb's] feet have trodden shall be thine inheritance, and thy children's for ever, because thou hast wholly followed the Lord my God.

10 And now, behold, the Lord hath kept me [Caleb] alive, as he said, these forty and five years, even since the Lord spake this word unto Moses, while the children of Israel wandered in the wilderness: and now, lo, I am this day fourscore and five years old [or 85].

11 As yet I am as strong this day as I was in the day that Moses sent me: as my strength was then, even so is my strength now, for war, both to go out, and to come in.

12 Now therefore *give me this mountain,* whereof the Lord spake in that day; for thou heardest in that day how the Anakims were there, and that the cities were great and fenced: *if so be the Lord will be with me, then I shall be able to drive them out as the Lord said.*

13 And Joshua blessed him, and gave unto Caleb the son of Jephunneh Hebron for an inheritance.

14 Hebron therefore became the inheritance of Caleb the son of Jephunneh the Kenezite unto this day, *because that he wholly followed the Lord God of Israel.*

At 85 years of age, Caleb still had a conqueror's mentality. First, in verse 9, Caleb rehearsed to Joshua what God had promised him through Moses: "Surely the land whereon thy feet have trodden shall be thine inheritance, and thy children's for ever, because thou hast wholly followed the Lord my God" (*KJV*). Then after he reminded Joshua of God's promise, Caleb recounted the faithfulness of God: "And now, behold, the Lord hath kept me alive, as he said, these forty and five years, even since the Lord spake this word unto Moses, while the children of Israel wandered in the wilderness" (v. 10 *KJV*).

Lastly, Caleb resolved to do something about what God had said. Caleb was firm and resolute to possess that which God had promised him those many years before. Caleb declared, "As yet I am as strong this day as I was in the day that Moses sent me: as my strength was then, even so is my strength now, for war, both to go out, and to come in. Now therefore *give me this mountain*" (vv. 11–12 *KJV*)!

No one with a grasshopper mentality is going to conquer and overcome odds as Joshua and Caleb did. Notice these two men never said the odds weren't stacked against them, naturally speaking. They never denied the existence of those giants in the land of Canaan. *They simply refused to acknowledge the inhabitants' ability to keep them from receiving what God had promised!*

Joshua and Caleb had the mentality that they would not be defeated, and they would not quit. And what happened? They were not defeated. Instead, they conquered the enemy and received what God said was theirs.

Friend, as Christians, we need to get rid of any grasshopper mentality that has tried to hold us back and keep us in bondage. God was with Moses and Aaron, and He was with Joshua and Caleb. But because you are in Christ, God is with you too! And He said He would never leave you nor forsake you. Joshua and Caleb held on to their belief in God for 45 years. Yet, how many of us are ready to give up and quit believing God after 45 *days*? We start out standing strong, but before long, we're wondering where God went. We are even doubting His Word that says He would never leave us (Heb. 13:5).

Notice that for 40 years, Joshua and Caleb had to live among people who were unbelieving concerning the promises of God. Every day, they had to declare their faith or be swallowed up in the doubt and unbelief that others around them were speaking.

I can just imagine Caleb talking about taking his mountain, the land of Hebron, that God had said belonged to him and his descendants. I imagine that every day, he said, "I am going to take my mountain; I am going to take that land." Others were saying, "Would to God that we had stayed in Egypt. Would to God that we had died in this wilderness" (Num. 14:2). Friend, that was a defeatist attitude! And notice how God responded to it.

> **NUMBERS 14:11–12** (*KJV*)
> **11** And the Lord said unto Moses, How long will this people provoke me? and how long will it be ere they believe me, for all the signs which I have shewed among them?
> **12** I will smite them with the pestilence [or, will *permit* them to be smitten], and disinherit them, and will make of thee a greater nation and mightier than they.

Moses interceded on behalf of the people, saying, in effect, "If You allow these people to die here, it will be said of You back in Egypt that You slew them in the wilderness because You were not able to bring them into their own land" (see Num. 14:13–16).

The Lord answered Moses, saying, "Okay, they won't die of the pestilence or plague. But this generation will not see the promise. Because of their rebellion, they will not set foot in the land I promised. They will eventually die off, and I will bring their sons and daughters into the land" (vv. 20–35).

I want you to notice what happened to the Israelites who rebelled against God's promise and said that it couldn't be done. They got exactly what they said!

> **NUMBERS 14:27–30**
> **27** "How long will this wicked community grumble against me [the Lord]? I have heard the complaints of these grumbling Israelites.
> **28** So tell them, 'As surely as I live, declares the Lord, *I will do to you the very things I heard you say:*
> **29** In this desert your bodies will fall—every one of you twenty years old or more who was counted in the census and who has grumbled against me.
> **30** Not one of you will enter the land I swore with uplifted hand to make your home, except Caleb son of Jephunneh and Joshua son of Nun.'"

You see, when things got hard for those Israelites, they kept looking back. They kept saying, "Why did we ever leave Egypt anyway?" But you can never win with God by having that kind of attitude. Once you set out with the promise of God, don't ever talk about going back. Don't think about it—don't even look in that direction!

Wherever you are in walking out the promises of God, you are further along than when you first started. So keep looking at the promise. Stay focused on it. Develop the conqueror's mentality that says, "God said it. I believe it. And that settles it! I cannot be defeated, and I will not quit! I will possess my promised land!"

With that attitude, you *will* possess what God has promised. But you will have to be determined. The devil is not going to roll over and play dead just because you make a bold declaration. However, he *will* have to move out of your way because of the Word of God spoken in faith time and time again. The Word in your heart released in words—from your own lips—will produce power that no enemy can withstand.

The devil is not going to pay any attention to what you say just because you said it. But he will pay attention to what you say in faith based on God's Word. The devil doesn't fear you because of who you are in yourself. He fears you because of Whose you are and because of who you are in Christ—because you know who you are and what you can do in Him.

You see, the devil knows that if he can keep you in fear, doubt, and unbelief, he can keep you in an attitude of defeat. He can keep you in that grasshopper mentality and stop you from receiving by faith the abundant life that God has provided. But if you will rise up with the truth of God's Word on your lips, you will develop that conqueror's mentality that will cause you to enter into and live in the overflow blessings of God.

The Power of Choice

What are you waiting for? We've been looking at the experience of Joshua and Caleb and the children of Israel, but the "land" of abundance belongs to you in Christ today! Yet there are giants that will try to stand in your way too—not literal giants but obstacles and hindrances that are bigger than you are in yourself. You might feel limited. But you will have to conquer these giants just as the Israelites had to conquer their giants. And you will have to do it through your faith in God.

Let's look at a New Testament man of God who had a conqueror's mentality: the Apostle Paul. Paul wrote the following verses, which were written for our benefit, by the inspiration of the Holy Spirit.

> **ROMANS 8:31,37**
> **31** . . . If God is for us, who can be against us?
> **37** . . . we are more than conquerors through him who loved us.

> **2 CORINTHIANS 2:14**
> **14** But thanks be to God, who always leads us in triumphal procession in Christ and through us spreads everywhere the fragrance of the knowledge of him.

You see, the Promised Land for us today consists of those things God has provided for us in redemption. Jesus paid the price for salvation, and included in that salvation is our healing, our deliverance, our prosperity, our protection, and our well-being—spirit, soul, and body.

Some people believe that Heaven is our Promised Land. In fact, songs have been written and sung using such language as found in the old hymn written by Samuel Stennett: "On Jordan's stormy banks I stand, and cast a wishful eye to Canaan's fair and happy land where my possessions lie."[1]

But Heaven is not our Promised Land. The Israelites had to face giants—obstacles—to enter their Promised Land. But in Heaven, there won't be any enemies to conquer or battles to fight. Our battles are fought right here on the earth, because God wants us to enter into those things He has promised while we are here, not when we get to Heaven.

You see, Satan was defeated when Jesus rose from the dead and ascended on High to the right hand of the Father. But as long as we are on this earth, we are going to have to enforce that defeat. The enemy will try to come against us with thoughts, feelings, and suggestions that don't line up with the Word of God. What are we going to do? We're going to fight the good fight of faith! The Bible says the weapons of our warfare are not carnal but mighty through God for the pulling down of strongholds (2 Cor. 10:4). How do we pull down those strongholds of the enemy? "Casting down imaginations, and every high thing that exalteth itself against the knowledge of God, and bringing into captivity every thought to the obedience of Christ" (2 Cor. 10:5 *KJV*).

I want you to particularly notice that after God gave the Israelites the Promised Land, they, too, had a part to play. They had to go in and possess the land. God fulfilled His part when He made the promise. All they had to do was believe in the integrity and faithfulness of God, and as they acted on that belief, He did the rest.

Similarly, we have a part to play today in enjoying the promises of God. In His great plan of redemption, God has made available to us salvation, healing, and prosperity. Now we have to possess by faith what He has provided. If we're going to live in our Promised Land, in a land of abundance and overflow, we're going to have to do what the children of Israel did. We're going to have to trust and obey God.

Whether or not we will possess our promises is up to each of us. The choice is ours. We can allow circumstances to limit us and cause us to turn aside from believing God wholeheartedly, or we can rise up with the Word of God in our heart and in our mouth, and we can boldly say, "Give me this mountain! I believe that it shall be even as it was told me (Acts 27:25)!" We can adopt a grasshopper mentality and see ourself as weak, defeated, and a victim of circumstances, or we can develop a conqueror's mentality, refusing to allow circumstances to limit us or keep us from possessing everything that belongs to us in Christ.

How Big Is Your God?

I think you can already see that your attitude—your mentality—affects how you look at life's limitations. If you have a grasshopper mentality, you will see problems as big, even compared to God and what He can do for you. But with a conqueror's mentality, you will see those same problems as small compared to God. You will know that God is for you, and since He is for you, no one can stand successfully against you. You will know and be confident that what God said, He will surely do for *you*.

I once saw a movie about a young bear cub whose mother had been killed. The young bear bonded to a wise male Kodiak bear who became the young bear's protector, teacher, and friend. In one of the funniest scenes in the movie, this young cub is standing on his hind legs while a mountain lion that tried to attack the cub runs away in fear for its life. The little cub growls as ferociously as he can, thinking the mountain lion is running from him. But what the cub doesn't see standing just behind him is the giant Kodiak bear!

When you are confronted with the attacks of the enemy, see yourself facing the enemy in the power and authority of Jesus Christ, the ultimate Conqueror. When you stand your ground, speaking God's Word in faith, the enemy will turn from you and run in terror (James 4:7). You will become a "giant" in the realm of the spirit when God Almighty stands behind you. So get rid of any thoughts of failure or defeat and take hold of the thoughts of God. Why give up and *quit* when you can *conquer* instead?

---

[1]Samuel Stennett (1727–1795), "Promised Land (On Jordan's Stormy Banks I Stand)."

part two

How to Live Above Life's Limits

Living Large by Thinking Large!

Have you ever heard the phrase "living large"? Maybe you've heard someone say about another person, "Man, he's living large!"

What does it mean to "live large"? When someone is living large, he or she is living and experiencing something far above and beyond the normal standard for living. Well, God wants you, as His child, to live large too! But before you can live large *His* way, you must develop the *habit* of thinking large.

We've been looking at how our beliefs—our attitudes and mindsets affect the kind of life we will live on this earth. As Christians, we need to ask ourselves the question: Will we live beneath our rights and privileges in Christ, or will we live above life's limitations—in the overflow? The truth is, God wants us to

live in the overflow more than we want it! But we have to understand how to do it. It begins with preparation, with training your
mind in the *habit* of thinking like God thinks.

From Bondage to Abundance

Remember we read, *"These things happened to them* [the people
of Israel] *as examples and were written down as warnings for
us..."* (1 Cor. 10:11). We can learn from the example of the Israelites
in the Old Testament because this verse in First Corinthians says
that what happened to them was written for our benefit.

Although God's people, the children of Israel, were being held
captive as slaves in Egypt, God wanted them to enter into abundance. He wanted to lead them from that land, a place where
they literally had nothing, to the land of Canaan—their Promised
Land—where they would live in the overflow and enjoy an abundance of blessings.

For some background information, let's look at God's dealings
with Moses, God's chosen vessel to lead His people from bondage
to abundance, in Exodus chapter 3:

EXODUS 3:7–8
7 The Lord said [to Moses], "I have indeed seen the
misery of my people in Egypt. I have heard them
crying out because of their slave drivers, and I am
concerned about their suffering.
8 So I have come down to rescue them from the
hand of the Egyptians and to bring them up out
of that land into a good and spacious land, a land
flowing with milk and honey...."

Under Moses' leadership, God delivered the people out of the land of their captivity. Physically, they were free. But in their minds, they were still thinking like captive slaves. To help the Israelites change their thinking after their exodus from Egypt, Moses gave them instructions as he described to them the land of abundance and overflow to which God was leading them.

> **DEUTERONOMY 8:6–10**
> 6 Observe the commands of the Lord your God, walking in his ways and revering him.
> 7 For the Lord your God is bringing you into a good land—a land with streams and pools of water, with springs flowing in the valleys and hills;
> 8 a land with wheat and barley, vines and fig-trees, pomegranates, olive oil and honey;
> 9 a land where bread will not be scarce and you will lack nothing; a land where the rocks are iron and you can dig copper out of the hills.
> 10 When you have eaten and are satisfied, praise the Lord your God for the good land he has given you.

As we saw in the last chapter, that older generation of Israelites didn't enter the Promised Land because there were enemies in the land that they would have to defeat, and they couldn't see themselves conquering those enemies. They didn't obey the instruction Moses gave them. Of the original 12 spies, only two, Joshua and Caleb, could see themselves taking what God said already belonged to them.

Joshua and Caleb possessed a conqueror's mentality—one that enlarged their thinking to line up with God's way of thinking and embraced His will for their lives. And when that entire

generation of older Israelites died in the wilderness, Joshua and
Caleb remained to lead the younger generation into their land of
promise. They could see themselves doing what God said they
could do. They wouldn't back off of it, regardless of the opposition. And so they ended up living large by thinking large! They
had developed the *habit* of thinking large.

From 'Not Enough' to 'Just Enough' to 'More Than Enough'

I want you to notice that, all along, God intended to bring the
Israelites from bondage to abundance, from a land of "not enough"
to a land of "more than enough"! That's what God wants to do
for us today. He wants to bring us from a land where there's not
enough to a land where there's more than enough! But we have to
cooperate with Him so He can do it. Just as the children of Israel
had to obey God on their journey from one land to another, we
must obey Him and be doers of His Word today. We must change
our thinking until it lines up with God's thoughts. And then we
must *act* on His Word in faith.

As we saw, the Israelites' journey from Egypt to Canaan didn't
take place overnight. After they left Egypt, they spent some time
in the wilderness, where God supernaturally took care of them. He
gave them manna from Heaven and quail to eat, and He gave them
fresh water to drink. He even kept their clothes and shoes from
wearing out on their journey. Deuteronomy 29:5 says, *"During
the forty years that I led you through the desert, your clothes did
not wear out, nor did the sandals on your feet."* You see, the wilderness for the children of Israel was a land of "just enough."

Many Christians are in a land of just enough today—a land of just barely getting by. Others are in a land of not enough; their needs are not being met. Yet some have learned to change their thinking and their believing, and they have entered God's promised land for them—a land of more than enough, where they are living in abundance in the overflow blessings of God!

You're not living life to the full—life in the overflow—when there's *lack*. And neither are you living in the overflow when there's *just enough*! Living in the overflow is when there is more than enough to meet your needs and someone else's needs too! But no matter where you are today in your circumstances, you can be assured that God has more in store for you! Are you ready to move to the next level of abundance? If so, you have to be willing to change, or "enlarge," your thinking.

> **ISAIAH 54:2–3**
> 2 "Enlarge the place of your tent, stretch your tent curtains wide, do not hold back; lengthen your cords, strengthen your stakes.
> 3 For you will spread out to the right and to the left; your descendants will dispossess nations and settle in their desolate cities."

Let's discuss Isaiah 54:2 from the standpoint of the mind, because it has a prophetic application to the Church. This verse says, *"Enlarge the place of your tent, stretch your tent curtains wide, do not hold back; lengthen your cords, strengthen your stakes."* There's a lot of good teaching on receiving from God from the standpoint of the spirit, or heart, of man. And it's true: It is with the heart that a person believes (Rom. 10:10). But what about the mind? What you think on or meditate on will affect your heart, or spirit. Therefore, what you *think* can greatly affect what you *believe*. So you see, your mind has a lot to do with what you receive in life from God.

In the New Birth, our spirit is born again; it is made completely new. Second Corinthians 5:17 says, "Therefore if any man be in Christ, he is a new creature: old things are passed away; behold, all things are become new" (*KJV*). But despite the fact that the spirit of man is reborn in the New Birth, the mind and body are not automatically changed. That's why Paul wrote in Romans 12:1–2 that we are to present our body unto God as a living sacrifice and renew our mind with His Word. If we don't, since we are still in this world, we will fall back into our old way of behaving and believing.

In one way or another, the world is constantly trying to impose its limits on us by telling us what we can't have, can't do, can't be, and so forth. But God's Word tells us who we are in Christ, what we can do through Him, and what belongs to us because of Him!

Rise Above Small Thinking by Embracing the Thoughts of God

When God said to the Israelites, *"Enlarge the place of your tent"* (Isa. 54:2), what does that mean to us today? For one, it means to make room in your mind to embrace the thoughts of God, His abundance, and what He wants to do! It means you have to quit thinking small if you're going to *"spread out to the right and to the left"* as verse 3 promises. In other words, God wants you to increase, but you have to do something first: You have to change, or enlarge, your thinking.

To live large in a place of abundance and overflow, we must cultivate the habit of thinking large. Have you ever noticed how large God was thinking when He had the Temple built in Jerusalem? It was the most magnificent structure that had ever been built. No small thinking went into the construction of that building. Even the garments the priests wore were made according to God's elaborate, detailed specifications.

God has never had a small thought; He always thinks big! We need to train ourselves to think like He thinks by reading, studying, and meditating on His Word.

The Gift of Imagination

We know that when God said, "Enlarge the place of your tent," He was saying, "Broaden the scope of your thinking. *Enlarge your thinking.*" Now let's look at the second part of Isaiah 54:2: *"Stretch your tent curtains wide."* In other words, we need to stretch our imagination and lift our thoughts to a higher level.

Even in the world, proponents of positive thinking will say, "If you can imagine it, you can do it." Well, God gave us our imagination. And we can take that imagination, yield it to the Holy Spirit, and go places in God's Word that we have never been before. We can think higher and dream bigger than we ever thought possible! As you read the promises of God, you have to use your imagination to "see" yourself living in and enjoying those promises. With your imagination, you can see yourself with the fulfillment of those promises. You can focus your thoughts on the reality of the Word of God.

I read an account once of a minister of the Gospel who was driving down a beautiful street lined on both sides by grandfather oak trees. Along this majestic boulevard were many stately mansions. The minister quietly admired the elaborate architecture of the homes on that street and the colorful, immaculate landscaping surrounded by ornate gates of iron.

Finally, he said out loud, "I could never imagine myself living in one of those." Immediately, the Holy Spirit spoke up inside him, in his spirit, and said, *Then you never will.*

Your imagination is a gift from God! The enemy has tried to pervert the imagination by causing people to meditate and think on things that are impure and ungodly. But God gave each of us a means of seeing ourselves where He wants us to be before we ever get there. It's called imagination.

I often heard my father, Rev. Kenneth E. Hagin, say as he ministered healing to folks, "See yourself healed. See yourself doing what you couldn't do before!" That is the power of imagination— to see yourself in a better condition than you're in now so that, by faith, your life can begin to head in that direction.

Coaches often encourage their players to use their imagination too. Whether it's catching a pass, scoring a basket, or getting a great hit, coaches will say, "See yourself doing that."

Once I heard a successful race car driver say that before a race, he liked to take a few moments just to sit in his car before the drivers started their engines. He would place his hands on the steering wheel, close his eyes, and visualize the race. He would picture himself successfully taking corners, avoiding accidents, gaining speed and momentum, and winning the race!

What was this driver doing? He was using his imagination to see himself where he wanted to be. And this is what God wants each of us to do. He wants us to visualize ourselves possessing each promise and successfully overcoming every test, trial, and temptation along the way.

Your imagination is God's gift to you so you can see yourself where He wants you to be before you get there!

I will give you another illustration of the power of imagination. When I was a child, I remember going to the home of my mother's mother from time to time. She always had something special baked for us to eat when we arrived. There was a pineapple coconut cake that she often made, and it was out of this world!

On the way to Grandma's house, I would sit in the backseat of our car picturing that cake with white icing on it just sitting in the middle of Grandma's table. We could be 100 miles away from Grandma's, but I could envision the coconut that she sprinkled all over that cake. I could just see the crushed pineapple filling oozing between those layers. Many people have used Grandma's recipe, but it seems that no one can make that cake like Grandma made it!

There were times when we would stop by Grandma's just to say hello. Dad would be traveling to or from a meeting, so we would just drop by to visit for a bit. Grandma didn't know we were coming, but she always had some homemade teacakes in her cookie jar. Those teacakes were big and round and covered with sugar—and, boy, they were good! Every time I left Grandma's house, I left with a big bag of those teacakes.

My imagination was seeing that pineapple coconut cake or those teacakes before we ever arrived at Grandma's house. And although my grandmother went home to be with the Lord over 20 years ago, I still remember the things she baked as though it were yesterday. I can almost taste that cake and those teacakes now—I remember them that vividly!

Similarly, God wants us to use our imagination to see the fulfillment of His promises in our lives before they are actually manifested. Your imagination is God's gift to you, where the photographs, so to speak, of God's abundance are developed in your mind.

The dreams God gives you are not impossible or unreachable. Luke 1:37 says, "For with God nothing is ever impossible and no word from God shall be without power or impossible of fulfill-ment" (*Amplified*). So whatever God has put in your heart to have or do, meditate on it; don't ever let that word or that dream die. Keep it alive in your heart by "stretching your tent curtains wide." Whatever it is you are thinking about having or doing, you can go there with God and the Holy Spirit!

'Do Not Hold Back!'

The next part of Isaiah 54:2 says, *"Do not hold back."* Do not relinquish the power of your imagination. Don't strangle your imagination and your thoughts, hopes, and dreams from God's Word. Instead, use every opportunity to meditate on the possibili-ties and promises of God!

Natural circumstances will try to throttle your faith. But you need to continue to let your imagination soar! Circumstances will try to put a stranglehold on your dreams. But we're not to allow circumstances to limit us and hold us back! We're to continue to meditate on the promises of God and allow our thinking to become enlarged. And that enlarged thinking will produce something powerful, because no word of God is ever without power or impossible of fulfillment.

Remove the Restrictions of Your Mind

My son, Craig, owns a little race car with a 600-cc motorcycle engine. But there is a class of race car engine called the restrictor class, and in that class, the air-and-fuel flow to the carburetor is restricted. So a 300-cc engine, for example, with a restricted flow would be approximately a 225-cc engine.

Have you ever watched a NASCAR race? At certain race sites, such as Daytona, restrictor plates are fitted on top of the car's manifold where the carburetor sits. The plate covers the holes in the carburetor and restricts the airflow so the engine can't handle as much fuel. Therefore, the engine can't produce as much horsepower.

I like to use that natural illustration to show people what the devil tries to do to believers. Because the devil hasn't been able to stop some Christians from receiving from God, he tries to restrict them so that they're not receiving everything God has for them. They're enjoying life, all right, but they're not having it to the full, till it overflows!

But as we begin to trust and obey God and His Word, we begin to loosen that "restrictor plate" in our lives. We begin to line up our thoughts with God's thoughts and His way of thinking. Then with the help of the Holy Spirit, we put God's Word deep into our hearts, meditating on the promises and possibilities that we have in God. We grow strong, increasing in the strength and power of God. And we refuse to hold back and limit God! We enlarge ourselves—our thoughts and imagination—to receive and live in God's overflow!

Don't ever let the devil throttle your faith. It's important to know how he throttles people in their thinking and their believing, because we are not to be ignorant of his devices or schemes (2 Cor. 2:11).

The Chokehold of Selfishness

One way believers are throttled in their thinking is by having a stingy, beggarly attitude. They allow small thinking to rob them of the overflow blessings of God. They look only at their needs and at what they can get, instead of what they can give. They can't imagine themselves having abundance and being a blessing to others, because their thinking and believing are throttled. Their small ideas hinder them from receiving and walking in God's best.

The Chokehold of Pleasing Others Instead of God

Another way believers can be throttled in their thinking is through the opinions of others. We must learn to disregard negative criticism, because if we don't, it will hinder us from receiving from God.

No one likes to be criticized for what he believes. But if you want to receive from God, you must *think* right in order to *believe* right. And then you must *speak* right. In other words, you're going to have to say the right things; you're going to have to speak in line with God's Word even if it means going against popular opinion. That's what Joshua and Caleb did. When the 10 unbelieving spies said, "We're not able," Joshua and Caleb said, "We are *well* able!" (Num. 13:30)!

Joshua and Caleb went against the limiting popular opinion expressed by the other spies, because the opinion of those 10 spies was one of doubt and unbelief. Joshua and Caleb were exceedingly blessed because they refused to be limited by the opinions of others. God allowed them to enter the Promised Land, where they lived out their days in overflow blessings!

The Chokehold of Jealousy

You can also become throttled in your thinking by being jealous or envious of someone else. You need to make a decision that when thoughts of jealousy or envy come to your mind, you're not going to allow those thoughts to linger. When someone else gets blessed, rejoice with him! You must have the attitude, *I rejoice that So-and-so is living a life of abundance. Praise God! I'm in line to receive my blessings too!*

The Chokehold of Unforgiveness

Yet another way to become throttled and limited in your thinking is by meditating on the jealousy and envy of others toward *you*. Some people will be upset with you because you're believing God for abundance. And when you begin to prosper, they will get even more upset. They are jealous or envious—they are throttled in their own heart and mind. But you can't let their wrong thinking poison your own mind. Don't dwell on the wrongdoing of others. You'll then be free in your mind and heart to think on and believe the promises of God.

The Missing Link

Our text, Isaiah 54:2, goes on to say, *"Lengthen your cords."* We could liken lengthening our cords to lengthening our thoughts until they touch the thoughts of God. We are to stretch and lengthen our thoughts until they touch and take hold of the promises and blessings of God!

Have you ever seen a dog tied up with a rope or chain? A dog that's bound to a chain is so limited in movement that if someone put its food just beyond the length of that chain, the dog would eventually starve to death. Technically, that person is feeding the dog in the sense that he or she is putting food in a bowl and setting it out for the dog. But if the food is always put beyond the dog's reach, the dog will eventually die unless someone moves its food closer or lengthens its chain.

Have you ever felt as if the blessings of God were always just beyond your reach? Your thought life may be your missing link! Renewing your mind and changing your thinking to God's way of thinking will "lengthen your cords," as Isaiah 54:2 says, and enable you to possess and enjoy what has eluded you in the past.

I want to illustrate the point here that *thoughts are the links that form the chain that determines the level of existence and achievement we reach in this life.*

Our thought life is our link! Think about that! As you begin to meditate on and think in line with God's Word, you are putting links in the chain, so to speak. Abundance is available to us, but the devil has had many believers on a short chain. They haven't expanded their thinking and lengthened their cords to be able to take hold of the blessings of God.

Strengthen Your Stakes

The last part of Isaiah 54:2 says, *"Strengthen your stakes."* One way to strengthen your stakes is to be strong and courageous in your thought life. In other words, even after you've grasped the truth of God's Word and you have the understanding that God wants you to prosper and live in His overflowing blessings, you still have to continually deepen your understanding and fortify your mind with the Word of God.

The renewing of your mind that Paul talked about in Romans chapter 12 is a continual, ongoing process. As we saw in the last two chapters, you have to *persist* in building faith-based attitudes for increase. In other words, once you've built your faith up to receive for overflow, you must stand your ground, refusing to be moved or shaken from your faith.

You must determine to enlarge your thinking and not let anything limit or hinder you from receiving God's abundance. Remember, it's with the heart that a person believes—but believing begins in your thought life! A habit of thinking small will cause you to live small. But a habit of thinking large will cause you to live large in God!

I have heard people say, "Well, I know God has promised us a mansion in Glory, but I would be satisfied with just a little cottage." In fact, there is an old song that contains the words, "Lord, build me just a cabin in a corner of gloryland."[1]

Well, I can admire the dedication of people who feel that way, because what they are actually saying is, "I would love and serve God even if He didn't give me His many blessings." The only problem with that is that He *did* give us His many blessings! He recorded them in the pages of His Word, and He intends that we appropriate every one of them for His glory. I have read the Bible many times all the way through from Genesis to Revelation, and I have never seen anything in there about any cabins in Glory. I've read about mansions and sparkling streets of gold and gates made of a single pearl, but I've never read anything about a cabin or a cottage.

Certainly, a person has a right to have a "cottage" mentality if he or she wants to. But as for me, I choose to love and serve God and live in the *overflow* blessings! I choose to enlarge my thinking and exercise my faith to receive *all* the promises God has given me.

As I said before, I know I won't get there overnight, and neither will you. But we can *grow* ourselves into the promises of God. We can learn to think right—in line with God's Word—and meditate on the Word until it *grows* on the inside of us, in our heart or spirit. When the Word becomes reality on the inside, it won't be long before it becomes reality on the outside.

I am reminded of a story about a couple who were in their 40s before they had a child. They became very financially well-off before the child was born. When the child was about three years old, his dad picked him up one day and, gently holding him in his arms, said, "I can't wait for you to grow up so I can show you my world."

That's what God wants for each of us! Similarly, He wants us to grow up and experience His world—His abundance where He lives large. As we renew our mind with His Word and grow in faith, we'll be able to live in that world, above life's limitations and in the overflow blessings of God.

---

[1] Curtis Stewart, "Lord Build Me a Cabin in Glory," © 1952 Fort Knox Music, BMI / Trio Music, BMI.

chapter 5

Living Beyond the Past

What hinders you from receiving God's best for your life? It is important to identify those hindrances so you can begin taking steps toward overcoming and living above them. In my almost 50 years in ministry, time and time again I have witnessed Christians missing out on blessings they should have been enjoying, because they were tormented with guilt concerning their past.

Some people can't see the life that's before them because of their past. In other words, they are allowing the past to limit them by obscuring their view of the future. They have not learned to let go and live beyond the limits of their past.

Others who have experienced past hurts and disappointments catch a glimmer of hope for a better future. But they have absolutely no idea how to get there. They allow their past to hinder them from making any progress toward their future.

Things that have happened in the past sometimes have a way of scarring people to the point that they excuse themselves from possibilities of a better future. But the Apostle Paul indicated that if you're going to have abundant life, you must live beyond the limits of your past.

> **PHILIPPIANS 3:13–14**
> 13 Brothers, I do not consider myself yet to have taken hold of it. But one thing I do: Forgetting what is behind and straining towards what is ahead,
> 14 I press on towards the goal to win the prize for which God has called me heavenwards in Christ Jesus.

Paul was a man who pursued the things of God with everything within him. He said, *"I press on towards the goal to win the prize for which God has called me heavenwards in Christ Jesus"* (v. 14). But notice that before he said anything about pressing toward the future, he also addressed the past. He said, *"Forgetting what is behind . . . ."*

Backward About Going Forward

Perhaps things from your past have caused you a lot of heartache and pain. You need to realize that, yes, you have a past, but there is a tomorrow in your life too! And it can be as bright as the promises of God. Yet it all hinges on what you do with the past. You have to *forget* what is behind you.

I once heard an old farmer say, "That mule is awfully backward about going forward." This is also true of many people! Concerning the past, I heard someone else say, "There's no use in looking back unless that's the direction you're planning to go." Another person said this (and I really like this one): "Don't waste a day regretting yesterday. Instead, spend your time making memories for tomorrow."

Everyone has to deal with a past. But God wants you to realize that *there is life beyond your past!* Your past cannot be changed. But your tomorrows *can* be changed by your actions *today.*

You may be asking, "Why is it so important to deal with the past?"

Because the prisons of the past will try to limit and keep you from living free today. God wants you to live free today and every day—in His fullness, His overflowing life!

Our Non-Existent Past

Just how do you "forget" the past? Number one, ask God to forgive you, and then realize that, because of the sacrifice of Jesus, the past doesn't exist anymore (Micah 7:18–19; Ps. 103:12; 1 John 1:7,9). It's over and done. The only place the past really exists is in our memories.

In the mind of God, your past no longer exists. So don't dwell on it. If you do, it will hinder you from moving successfully toward the future God has in store for you. The devil would have you think that you have to turn around and do battle with the past. But in reality, the past is gone. If you allow him to engage you in battling the ghosts of your past, you will become distracted from enjoying the victories of the future.

The enemy will try and chase you with your past. It's only when you turn to look back at it that he can catch you. The devil doesn't have any new tricks. He uses your memories of the past to try to hound you. He tries to chase you down with thoughts of the past so that you will relive it. He uses the same evil scheme on everyone over and over again.

Have you ever watched a dog chase every car that goes by on the street? That dog hasn't caught a car yet (and I wonder what would it do with a car if it ever *did* catch one?). But he continues to chase every single one that passes. That's all it knows to do, so it does the same thing over and over again.

Of course, the weaknesses of our flesh have made our past imperfect. And our immature behavior has robbed us of many a success. But, thank God, the failures of the past have no effect on today if we're walking with God. Walking with Him, we don't have a past riddled with failures; we have a future bright with the promises of God.

Why do we insist on living so much in the past? One reason is that the devil is the "god of this world" (2 Cor. 4:4), and he uses the sense realm—thoughts, feelings, and suggestions—to try and bring our focus and attention toward our mental "photographs" of the past. If a person has asked forgiveness, the things he or she did in the past don't exist as far as God is concerned. They are only photographs, or memories, that the enemy would like a person to meditate on and hold in memory.

The devil realizes that if he can get us to remain captive to the limitations of our past, then the best we can produce are going to be excuses. Many people have a thousand reasons why their past is keeping them from being a success today. The enemy understands that if he can keep them from looking at tomorrow in the light of God's Word, he can limit them from being the success God has called each one of them to be.

It might help you to point to yourself each day and say out loud: "God has called me to be a success. He has said that I am to have life and live it to the full. I intend to do just that!"

Failures Are Not Final!

Some people are truly imprisoned by their past. They feel that it is impossible to enjoy life or have even a tiny measure of success because of everything that has happened. But, friend, *failures are not final!* Your past is never the end of your life's story. Let me tell you the rest of the story by sharing some insights from the lives of people in the Bible who had difficult pasts to overcome.

Abraham, who is known as the father of faith, was a man with a past that he left behind to fully follow God. The Lord told Abraham, *"Leave your country, your people and your father's household and go to the land I will show you"* (Gen. 12:1). So Abraham left his family and friends. He headed out to find the land God was sending him to, even though he wasn't exactly sure where that land was! God just said to *go*, and Abraham *went*! Of course, we know that during Abraham's lifetime, he walked intimately with God and became one of the most successful men of his time.

Notice that as he set out to obey God, we never read about Abraham longing to return to his roots or even thinking about his homeland. God was taking him to a new homeland that He planned to give to Abraham and his lineage forever. Abraham was successful because he refused to look back. He set his face toward the future with God, knowing that the future God had planned for him had nothing to do with his past or where he came from.

Moses is another man in the Old Testament from whom we can learn. He grew up in the Pharaoh's house in Egypt with all the riches of the palace at his disposal. Yet, when he finally got in line with God's plan to use him to deliver all of Israel out of Egyptian slavery, Moses got the job done without ever looking back.

Now, in the case of Moses, at first he got ahead of God. He tried to take justice into his own hands and got himself in trouble—so much so that he had to flee Egypt and live on the backside of the desert for many years.

Then Moses had a confrontation with God in the burning bush (Exod. 3:2), and he was not so quick this time to try to bring justice to the people of Israel. He wasn't necessarily looking back and remembering the past; Moses was simply making excuses for why God could never use him to accomplish such a feat. However, we know that, ultimately, God was able to use Moses to lead some two to three million Israelites out of Egypt and to the brink of a new homeland of promise.

In the New Testament, looking at the life of Peter, we see a man who denied Christ three times. Peter had committed his life to following Jesus and serving Him. But at the time Jesus was crucified, Peter's actions were so shameful that he doubted God could ever use him. Yet, we know that Peter went on to lead 3,000 people to Christ in one day (Acts 2:41) and became one of the staunchest leaders of the Early Church.

And what about the Apostle Paul, who was first known as Saul of Tarsus, a zealous persecutor of the Church? We read in Acts 22:20 that Paul consented to the death of Stephen. Paul had no doubt consented to the punishment, torture, imprisonment, and death of many believers in Jesus Christ. But then something happened. Paul, or Saul, came face to face with the glory of God. He had an encounter with the One he had so ignorantly persecuted.

Afterward, what was Paul to do with his past? He told us in Philippians 3:13 and 14: *"Forgetting what is behind and straining toward what is ahead, I press on toward the goal to win the prize for which God has called me heavenward in Christ Jesus."*

Paul had to forget a lot—all of his past mistakes and wrong-doings against God Himself. Paul had to forget how much he had come against the things of God.

But let's look at something else Paul had to forget. Not only did he have to forget the wrongs he'd committed, he had to forget about his past status. Paul had been a successful and highly regarded leader in the religious community. In one scripture, Paul referred to himself before he came to Christ as *"a Hebrew of Hebrews; in regard to the law, a Pharisee"* (Phil. 3:5). He was a member of an elite class of religious leaders. Paul was a man who had to forget his associations and his friends to follow his future with God.

At some point, every person on the planet must make the choice either to accept a future with God, where he can have life more abundantly, or to live in the past with its limitations, disappointments, and failures. All of us have some kind of baggage from the past. But consider the baggage Paul could have carried from his past had he chosen to. If anyone could excuse himself from having a future with God because of his past, it was Paul!

God does not use only people who have a so-called perfect past. He also uses people who rise above their past to follow Him. God can change a person so that he is no longer a reflection of his past. God can enable him to move beyond what he has experienced in the past to live for Him today and experience His overflow blessings.

God is not looking for perfect people, *because there are no perfect people!* God is looking for those who have accepted the blood sacrifice of Jesus, the only perfect One to ever walk the face of this earth.

So how does a person with a troubled past take hold of his future with God? In the remainder of this chapter, I will share with you four ways not just to forget the past, but to live beyond it and enjoy a prosperous future in the overflow blessings of God.

Number One: Change What You Identify With!

The first thing you must do to live beyond your past after you have changed your identity by becoming "a new creature in Christ" is *to identify with that change.*

> ### 2 CORINTHIANS 5:17 (KJV)
> 17 Therefore if any man be in Christ, he is a new creature: old things are passed away; behold, all things are become new.

It's important to understand that if you have been born again, you are *in Christ*. You have a new identity. You are no longer the person you once were. You are a new person in Christ. What did

Paul say to "behold" or focus on? Your *new* identity in Christ! You should only identify with the things of God, not with the things of the past. The "old man"—your old, unregenerate nature—no longer exists!

My father sometimes told stories of hanging around friends as a young boy before he was saved and before he became bedfast. Sometimes they would pick locks on buildings just for fun. He said he could pick almost any lock of that day.

One day after he had gotten saved and was raised off the bed of affliction, he saw some of those same old friends talking together on a street corner. He stopped to chat with them, and one of them brought up one of those lock-picking incidents and asked, "Hey, Kenneth, do you remember that?"

He answered him, "No, I don't remember that. The guy who did that died."

Another one said, "Oh, Kenneth, you were there. And that's you standing here now."

He said again, "No, the guy who did that died."

One of the friends insisted, "We know you were sick and you almost died. But you *didn't* die."

He said, "I know, but the man who did those things *has* died." And he took that opportunity to talk about the Word of God and share the Gospel.

My dad knew who he was in Christ. He never identified with the old, unsaved man but with the new man, re-created in Christ. You must learn to do the same. When somebody tries to get you to focus on the past, you can say, "The person who did that is dead. I am living beyond my past! As far as God is concerned, my past doesn't exist anymore. It is gone forever."

If you don't focus on who you are in Christ and on your future with God, the devil will constantly remind you of your past—of everything you ever did that was wrong. He will try to discourage and intimidate you. He will say things such as, "You'll never make it. You'll never fulfill that dream. Just look at your past. Look at all the bad things you've done."

You don't even have to address those things the devil is reminding you of. All you have to do is say, "The person who did that is dead. I am a new creature in Christ!"

Number Two:
Understand the Power of the Blood!

The second thing you must do to focus on the future and live beyond your past is to realize and accept the fact that your past is under the blood of Jesus. First John 1:9 says, *"If we confess our sins, he is faithful and just and will forgive us our sins and purify us from all unrighteousness."* God is not keeping track of your sins. If you have confessed those sins, He has wiped your slate clean.

Regardless of what you may have done yesterday, you can have a clean slate today. It seems people are always talking about what they did yesterday. What you did yesterday can't be changed, but what you do tomorrow can.

In order to successfully let go of yesterday and take hold of the possibilities of tomorrow, you must learn to forgive as God forgives. And that includes forgiving *yourself*! If you've confessed your mistakes and sins, God has forgiven you. Now *you* need to forgive you!

Living with the guilt of the past will hinder your faith—your ability to receive from God and walk in His best. That's why it is absolutely necessary that you let go of the guilt of the past and receive God's forgiveness.

Number Three:
Don't Cater to Your Past—Neglect It!

The third thing you must do to live beyond your past and live focused on the promises of God for your future is to neglect your past. We know that we have to "forget those things that are behind us" as the Apostle Paul wrote in Philippians 3:13. One definition for the word "forget" in that verse is *to neglect*. You have to choose to neglect your past, to leave it alone. Don't coddle it or care for it—don't even think about it. *Neglect* it!

Paul went on in Philippians 4:8 to list what we *are* to think on—what we *should* pay attention to and *not* neglect!

> **PHILIPPIANS 4:8**
> 8 Finally, brothers, whatever is true, whatever is noble, whatever is right, whatever is pure, whatever is lovely, whatever is admirable—if anything is excellent or praiseworthy—think about such things.

The things of your past that are hindering you from God's best today don't fit the criteria in this verse of what you are to think on. There is no value at all to holding on in your thoughts to those things of the past. They will limit you. So forget them. Choose to neglect them, caring only for the things you have with God—for what He says about your future.

Number Four: Focus on the Future!

Once you begin neglecting the past, what else do you need to do? Just simply forgetting the past is not enough. The fourth thing you must do to live beyond your past is to embrace the future.

Do you know why many people don't embrace the future? It's because they don't understand that God has a bright future planned for them. Others are reluctant to step out in faith and fully embrace the future because, although they know God has a plan, they only see a part of the plan; they don't see everything.

But God is not going to show you the whole plan at once, because the Bible says that the just shall live by faith (Rom. 1:17; Gal. 3:11; Heb. 10:38). So you must take the future one faith step at a time. Every time you take a step forward, the enemy is going to try and get you to turn back. He'll say, for example, "Hey, have you forgotten about the past?"

You need to say to him, "*Yes!* I *have* forgotten about the past! I choose to neglect the past and embrace the future!"

What About Tomorrow?

The best way I know to live beyond the past and embrace the promises of God for your future is with your words—or with God's Word in your heart and in your mouth. I'm talking about your confession—your positive confession of God's Word concerning your life. You need to make a constant confession of your faith concerning your tomorrows.

Have you ever heard someone say, "Well, I just don't know about tomorrow. I don't know whether I'm going to make it or not"?

That's exactly what the devil wants us to do. He wants us to be fearful and uncertain concerning our future. Jesus came to give us life more abundantly, but we have to do our part to receive that abundant life. You see, our confession will either put us over or keep us down and defeated. If we are going to walk in the abundant life Jesus came to give, we are going to have to talk about it.

Our confession of faith concerning the future should sound something like this: "I am a new creature in Christ. I am the righteousness of God in Him. I *will* fulfill the will of God for my life. No weapon formed against me will prosper. God gave me His best in the Person of His Son, Jesus. I accept and receive the full, abundant life He came to bring. And my future is bright with promise!"

Your confession will take you into the future or keep you living in the past. Mark 11:23 backs that up. If you believe something in your heart and you confess it with your mouth, believing that those things you say will come to pass, you will have whatever you say.

> MARK 11:23 (*NKJV*)
> 23 For assuredly, I say to you, whoever says to this mountain, "Be removed and be cast into the sea," and does not doubt in his heart, but believes that those things he says will be done, he will have whatever he says.

You see, your confession will take you successfully into the future or keep you chained to your past. You will have whatever you say. So use the words of your mouth to create a future instead of bemoaning the past. With your mouth, you can create a bright future or remain imprisoned by the past.

You're not embracing the future and focusing on God's overflowing blessings when you continually think and talk about the past. Have you ever seen someone walking down the street while looking back at something? Then, all of a sudden—*bam!*—he runs right into something or someone else. What happened? He was looking in the wrong direction. He was looking backward when he should have been looking forward.

If you want to walk into your future on a clear path, you must keep your focus on what's in front of you, not what's behind you. The enemy will try to get you to turn around and look back. You have to make up your mind once and for all that you're going to walk into the future with God. You're going to have to identify with the fact that you are a Christian, a new creature in Christ. You must understand the power of the blood of Jesus on your behalf to cleanse you from all unrighteousness. And you're going to have to embrace the future, focusing on the promises of God.

You may be thinking, *That all sounds good. But what right do I really have to expect a bright future when I have made so many mistakes in life?*

You have every right because of Jesus! And because He lives today, you have everything you need to go forward and take your future by storm. How can I make such a bold statement? Because of Jesus!

HEBREWS 4:14–15
14 Therefore, *since we have a great high priest* who has gone through the heavens, *Jesus the son of God, let us hold firmly to the faith we profess.*
15 For we do not have a high priest who is unable to sympathise with our weaknesses, but we have one who has been tempted in every way, just as we are—yet was without sin.

Not only has Jesus secured our eternal salvation, He ever lives to make intercession for us today—right now (Heb. 7:25). We have Someone pleading our case for us! We have Someone sitting at the right hand of the Father, Who pleads on our behalf.

In modern language, we might say it like this: "Jesus, our Attorney, sits next to the Judge, arguing our case for us."

Imagine Jesus saying on your behalf today, "Father, I paid the price for My client's freedom. He is coming to You by way of the blood. He deserves everything I purchased for him in My death, burial, and resurrection."

Then imagine the Judge rapping His gavel and saying, "All right, Counsel—Son—that will be Your client's judgment. He gets to live life to the full!"

Clearly, the Lord has made a way for you to live beyond the limitations of your past. Are you ready to do it? Sometimes forgetting the past is easier said than done. But it is absolutely necessary that you learn to let go. With God's help, you can do it! Your yesterdays may not be pretty, but God can make your tomorrows beautiful. Tomorrow with its sunrise awaits you. You must learn to answer it with grace, leaving the darkness of the past behind. There is Sonlight in your future! Jesus the Son of God died and lives forevermore so that your future might be secure. He will light your way and give you a tomorrow that is aglow with His abundant life.

Living Free in the 'Here and Now'

In John 10:10, Jesus said, "I came that they may have and enjoy life, and have it in abundance (to the full, till it overflows)" (*Amplified*). When was Jesus talking about our having life in abundance, till it overflowed? In *this* life. Jesus was talking about *today*—about *right now*!

In the last chapter, we talked about the past as a hindrance to living in the overflow. In this chapter, we're going to talk about the present, the "here and now." *Today* is the day of God's abundance! *Today*, God wants us to enjoy life to the full, till it overflows.

Nineteenth-century statesman Benjamin Disraeli once said, "Every day, man crucifies himself between two thieves: the regrets of yesterday and the fears of tomorrow."

As we saw in the last chapter, we can't afford to remain focused on the regrets of the past. But we also can't afford to live in fear of the future. I am by no means saying it's wrong to look at the future. Certainly, we need to plan for and work toward it. And we should look forward to the future with great anticipation. But we don't need to focus so much on the future *or* the past that we can't enjoy today.

Psalm 118:24 says, *"This is the day* [today, not some other day] *the Lord has made; let us rejoice and be glad in it."* This verse is talking about the day in which we live, the day and age of grace. But we need to take that same attitude toward every new day we experience every 24 hours.

Some people rejoice in *yesterday*. They're always talking about the "good old days." And some people are always waiting for *someday*. Some are looking so far into the future that they relegate all of their blessings to Heaven or to the "Sweet By-and-By." But God's Word says, *"Today* is the day to rejoice and be glad!"

God's 'Today' for You

You see, God has designed a plan for you *today*! Today, God wants you to step into that plan. Today, He wants you to begin living above the limitations of life and enjoying all His benefits. Today is the day of salvation. Today is the day of healing. Today is the day of deliverance. Today is the day of provision. Today is the day of overcoming and of going on to spiritual maturity. Today is the day of victory and success!

Today has great value. But we must take advantage of the opportunity it presents. If we don't, the promise of today will be of no value to us. Similarly, the Word of God is full of promises that pertain to life and godliness. But unless we take advantage of them, those promises won't benefit us.

> **HEBREWS 3:13-19**
> 13 But encourage one another daily, as long as it is called *Today,* so that none of you may be hardened by sin's deceitfulness.
> 14 We have come to share in Christ if we hold firmly till the end the confidence we had at first.
> 15 As has just been said: "*Today,* if you hear his voice, do not harden your hearts as you did in the rebellion."
> 16 Who were they who heard and rebelled? Were they not all those Moses led out of Egypt?
> 17 And with whom was he angry for forty years? Was it not with those who sinned, whose bodies fell in the desert?
> 18 And to whom did God swear that they would never enter his rest if not to those who dis-obeyed?
> 19 So we see that they were not able to enter, because of their unbelief.

The children of Israel were not able to enter into and possess the promise of God because of their unbelief. They hardened their hearts and refused to go into the Promised Land. And they died in the wilderness as a result of their missed opportunity to believe God and take Him at His Word.

Likewise, many people today, because of unbelief, are not able to enter into the things that God has for them. But as Christians, we cannot afford to disbelieve for one minute what God has said in His Word. We must be faithful in the here and now, believing God and appropriating His promises today.

Someone said, "That's very simplistic." Well, it may be. I never said that believing the Word of God was difficult. Human reasoning and the flesh seem to make it hard. But simply taking God at His Word is the easiest thing in the world to do!

Obey Today

Let's look again at Hebrews 3:15: *"As has just been said: 'Today, if you hear his voice, do not harden your hearts as you did in the rebellion.'"* Notice that the writer of Hebrews is challenging us. He says that when we hear God's voice, we should obey it *today*! When we receive revelation from God's Word, He wants us to be doers of His Word instantly, not sometime in the future.

In this scripture, God is saying, "Don't be like the children of Israel who hardened their hearts and disobeyed Me." Those Israelites were too taken up with the bondage of the past and were too afraid of the future to trust God in the present, in the here and now.

Someone might ask, "Well, didn't God promise the Israelites that Promised Land? If He promised it, why didn't He just give it to them? Why didn't He just bring them into the land? Why did they have to wander around in the wilderness for 40 years?"

When God promised the children of Israel the land of Canaan as their Promised Land, He *did* just give it to them! He told them it belonged to them and that He was bringing them into the land.

But they didn't believe Him. They took one look at all the obstacles standing in their way and doubted God could or would make His Word good to them.

As I said earlier, doubt and unbelief are why some people are not receiving from God today. Yes, they have read certain promises in the Word. They may have even believed those promises at one time. But then situations and circumstances that were contrary to those promises began to rise up and oppose them. And guess what? They backed off the promises. They backed off their faith in God's Word, and the victory was lost to them when it should have been won.

It's Still Not Too Late!

If that describes you, *today* is the day to pick those promises back up and meditate on them until they become a part of you. Begin today to speak those promises out loud until they begin registering on your heart, or spirit. Then keep on speaking them until you see that which you have believed. But start *today*.

Parents, teachers, and others in positions of authority have tried to instill in us this kind of "right now" attitude. For example, have you ever heard your mother or father assign you some task and then say, "Do it *right now*"?

Spiritually speaking, some people put off believing the Word of God. They have an "I'll-get-to-that-later" attitude. Maybe they are just hoping something will come to pass without their having to put too much effort into believing for it.

I don't know about you, but putting things off until later has never worked well for me. Even growing up, my procrastinating about something never went over big with my parents. For example, when my mother said, "Ken, wax the kitchen floor," she didn't mean I could opt to do it now or later. She didn't mean I could put it off until it was convenient for me.

When I was growing up, the floors in our house were made of linoleum. To wax them, you had to get down on your hands and knees and coat them using paste wax and a rag. Then when that coat dried, you had to get back down on the floor and buff it off with a clean rag.

Waxing the kitchen floor was no small chore, and I wasn't always eager to do it. But when Mama said, "It's time to wax the floor," I never said, "Okay, I'll do it next week." No, I did it right then, when she asked. In fact, I knew that every other Saturday, I was going to be waxing the kitchen floor, period!

If you're like me, when your parents asked you to do something, you knew that they wanted it done right then. They wouldn't accept your putting it off. So what makes us think that procrastinating is going to work with our Heavenly Father? He wants us to believe Him *today*. He wants us to trust Him *today*. Don't limit God just to the past or future. He wants us to praise and thank Him *today*. He wants us to enter into His overflow blessings by faith *today*.

We are to believe God while we have the opportunity. Jesus said in Luke 18:8, *"When the Son of Man comes, will he find faith on the earth?"* When are we to walk and live by faith? While we are on the earth, of course. And since we don't know the time of His coming, we are to walk by faith *today*!

Making the Most of the Present Will Ensure God's Best in Your Future

Some Christians have the notion that if they believe God for something, it should happen right away. Then if it doesn't, they give up and quit. It's important that we realize that our actions today open the doors of opportunity tomorrow. We have been waiting for opportunities to come tomorrow, or someday, instead of acting on what we believe today. We have been waiting on God when we should have been confessing God's Word that cannot and will not fail us if we'll hold fast to it.

And when do we hold fast to it? *Today!*

How you believe God today will affect what you receive from him tomorrow. Unbelief kept the Israelites out of their Promised Land for 40 years. An entire generation of Israelites had to die off before God could find a group of people who would take Him at His Word so He could show them His power.

Now Is the Time

Unbelief kept the Israelites out of the Promised Land, and unbelief will keep us out of our promised land today. But God has secured for you a bright future filled with His blessings and goodness. He has done it through Jesus Christ, Who paid a great price to save us from eternal damnation, heal our physical bodies, deliver us from every bondage, and prosper us financially and materially. These things are all available to us today in the here and now!

2 CORINTHIANS 6:2

2 For he says, "In the time of my favor I heard you, and in the day of salvation I helped you." I tell you, *now* is the time of God's favor, *now* is the day of salvation.

Another translation says, "Now the day of deliverance has dawned!" *Now* is our day of deliverance. And *right now* is the time for us to take hold of, and begin walking in, the blessings of God.

As I said before, many people want to relegate the blessings of God to the Sweet By-and-By—to when they get to Heaven. But look at the last part of First Timothy 4:8.

1 TIMOTHY 4:8

8 . . . godliness has value for all things, holding promise for *both the present life and the life to come.*

Let's read that same verse in the *New King James Version.*

1 TIMOTHY 4:8 (*NKJV*)

8 . . . godliness is profitable for all things, having promise of *the life that now is and of that which is to come.*

According to this verse, godliness is not just profitable in Heaven or in the Sweet By-and-By. It is also profitable in *this* life. Some people are always talking about the blessings they will receive once they get to Heaven. They take words from certain old-time Pentecostal songs and say, "We're just wanderers down here, traversing life's road, filled with tears and sorrow." And they talk about how it will all be different once they reach the "other side," meaning Heaven.

Well, thank God, Heaven will be different. And it will be a great day when we get there. I'm looking forward to that day! But if Heaven was our only "Canaan" or Promised Land, why does the Bible talk about overcoming obstacles and hindrances in connection to possessing the Promised Land? Remember, the children of Israel had to overcome giants in a land of walled cities before they could enjoy God's promised blessing. But we already know that in Heaven, there won't be any enemies to withstand. We have to withstand enemies *here and now* to enjoy God's blessings *here and now*!

God wants us to live the abundant life that Jesus purchased for us. He has given us a little bit of Heaven to go to Heaven in. That is an established fact. But it takes faith to receive it.

Maybe you haven't done all you should have with God's promises. But it's not too late to begin believing in the faithfulness of God.

> **HEBREWS 4:1–3**
> 1 Therefore, since the promise of entering his rest still stands, let us be careful that none of you be found to have fallen short of it.
> 2 For we also have had the gospel preached to us, just as they [the Israelites] did; but the message they heard was of no value to them, because those who heard did not combine it with faith.
> 3 Now we who have believed enter that rest . . . .

You can begin exercising your faith in God's Word *today* if you're not already doing so. You don't have to wait another minute. Now is the time!

"But I've tried that," somebody said, "and all I got was more problems."

But what do adverse circumstances have to do with God's Word? Absolutely nothing! The integrity of God's Word doesn't change, regardless of whether things look good or things look bad. The question should never be, "Will God make good on His Word?" Rather, the question should be, "What will you do with the Word? Will you be faithful to it, or will you endure for a while and then begin disbelieving it?"

The root of the Israelites' problems wasn't that they happened to see giants in the land that God had said belonged to them. No, their problems started with their response to the giants. Their problems began when they refused to believe and act on God's promise to them. Their unbelief plunged them into disobedience and, ultimately, failure for those who died in the wilderness and never saw the promise fulfilled.

We simply must not refuse to believe and act on God's Word today. Our faith in His Word is the vehicle that will transport us from where we are now in life to living the good life. Certainly, some people have a life of financial prosperity apart from faith in God's Word. But they're not living the abundant life—life to the full, to the maximum, till it overflows—that Jesus Christ provided.

People who are rich financially but are not walking with God live empty lives that are void of the love, joy, and peace of God. Their lives are void of real purpose and meaning, because there can be no real purpose in life for the one who is not trusting and obeying God and His Word.

No one can live the life Jesus purchased, except by the Word of God. Although some people reject the Word of God outright, did you know that a person can also live apart from the Word by simply reading or hearing it and then failing to act on it? For example, you might hear the Word and say, "Oh, that's good!" and then go on your way, mixing no faith with what you heard. In that case, you're not coming in line with the Word. You have separated yourself from it in terms of receiving any real blessing from it.

What Value Do You Place on the Word?

The value you place on the Word of God will determine the measure of blessing you receive from it. God has given us His Word and the ability to act on it. Now, what will we do with the Word of God?

Most Christians know that God's Word is His will. We understand that God's Word is God speaking to us. But do we really have the revelation in our heart that every word of God—every word in the Bible—can be utterly trusted?

How good is God's Word to you? Can it be trusted? Of course, it can be trusted, but do *you* trust it? How you answer that question will decide the value you place on God's Word.

My grandfather, my mom's dad, used to say to me, "Son, a person is only as good as his word." I was 12 years old when Paw-Paw went home to be with the Lord at the age of 70. But his words have stayed with me all these years.

In my grandfather's day, you didn't need an attorney to enter into agreements like you do now. He would say to me, "I don't have to have a lawyer. If I shake a man's hand and I say, 'This is what I'm going to do,' that is exactly what I'm going to do, even if it costs me something. If I have to take money out of my pocket, I'll do it. That's just the way it's going to be.'"

Well, holding my grandfather's words in mind, there are a lot of people on this planet today who are no good! I didn't say they weren't of any value, for God loved the whole world so much that He sent His only begotten Son to die for us (John 3:16). We are of great value to God! But there are many people today who *act* no-good. They lack character and integrity. Their words mean little or nothing. You can't trust them or place any value on what they say, because what they say and what they do don't always line up.

The Bible says that God is not a man that He should tell a lie (Num. 23:19). God stands behind every word He speaks. He can back up every word that proceeds from His mouth. He can be utterly trusted and depended upon. He never makes excuses or tries to weasel out of a promise. We can have confidence today that what He says, He does. He is good, and His Word is good.

Confidence 'For Such a Time as This'

Do you remember the account of Queen Esther? She was a Hebrew girl who was made the queen of a heathen king, King Ahasuerus, who reigned over more than 120 provinces from India to Ethiopia.

Even as the queen, Queen Esther was not permitted to approach King Ahasuerus' throne without being summoned. In other words, in that kingdom, unless the king sent for someone, that person could not just come into his presence unannounced or uninvited.

Esther was caught in a predicament because the fate of her people was at stake. Someone needed to intervene on their behalf quickly—*right then*. She ended up risking her life as she went to the king about the situation. Her cousin Mordecai had exhorted her, "Who knoweth whether thou art come to the kingdom *for such a time as this*?" (Esther 4:14 *KJV*). But God protected her as she bolstered her courage and sought the king's favor on behalf of her people.

There's a twofold lesson here. First, each one of us is on this earth "for such a time as this"—for the here and now. God has a plan and purpose for each one of us, and it is a good plan.

Second, although we in no way would compare a heathen king to God Almighty, the truth is, we can go boldly to the throne of the King of Kings and Lord of Lords without fear of harm or rejection. Because we are in Christ, we have been issued an open invitation to approach the throne of grace, where we may find God's help when we need it (Heb. 4:16).

HEBREWS 4:16
16 Let us then approach the throne of grace with confidence, so that we may receive mercy and find grace to help us in our time of need.

We don't have to stand at the door leading to the throne wondering if it's safe to go in. It is safe to enter! Not only that, God told us to enter with *confidence*. Some people feel they can't approach God in the here and now because of their past mistakes. But in Christ, we can be confident as we approach our Father God to talk to Him *today*.

If you are a parent or grandparent, perhaps you can relate to having your children or grandchildren approaching you with this kind of confidence. Just recently, I drove to the home of one of my young grandsons. As I was getting out of the car, he came running toward me, clutching his new billfold. "Poppy! Poppy! I want a dollar!" he yelled.

My grandson had his wallet out—he was ready to receive! There was no timidity in his request. Why? Because he knows he can come to me for anything. He's confident! He expected to get a dollar. And guess what? I gave him a dollar. What if he had asked me for *five* dollars? He would have gotten five dollars!

All my grandchildren approach me that way. When they come to visit, their parents barely get in the driveway before those boys are out of the car running toward our front door. They come right on in because they're confident. They know they are welcome at our house.

We can do the same thing with God. We can open the door, so to speak, run right in, and make our requests with confidence. And according to the Word of God, we will have the things that we desire of Him (1 John 5:14–15). Why don't more believers see they can approach God that way? It's thoroughly scriptural, but they have not renewed their mind to the fact that God wants them blessed, and He wants them blessed today. He wants them to approach Him today. He wants them to start believing and trusting Him today, *right now*.

Unfortunately, many Christians are not excited about "today." They've lost what I call their "first-day" attitude. Do you remember the attitude that you had the first day you accepted Christ and realized how much God loves you? You were full of joy, weren't you? What about the first day of your marriage? You were filled with enthusiasm and excitement about your spouse and all the possibilities you had to look forward to together. And what about the first day of your child's life—those first moments you laid eyes on that baby lying before you, so tiny and trusting?

If you'll learn to live every day with a first-day kind of attitude, you'll find that life is a whole lot more rewarding than you thought. You'll be able to live your life so full of energy and strength that you don't even think about the past. You are not regretting yesterday, begrudging today, or dreading tomorrow, because you're too busy rejoicing in today.

Your attitude about today is a choice you make. Today, you can begin living life to the full, till it overflows. Today, you can begin living victoriously above life's hindrances and limitations. Today is the day the Lord has made; you *can* rejoice and be glad in it. So make the choice to forget the past, to trust God for your future, and to live free today, in the here and now!

Standing Your Ground for Overflow (How to Catch a Thief)

We know that John 10:10 says, *"The thief comes only to steal and kill and destroy."* But just being aware of what the thief, the devil, has come to do doesn't make us automatically immune from his work in our lives Now, don't misunderstand me. We don't *have* to be stolen from, killed, or destroyed by the thief, but we must learn to keep him from doing these things in our lives.

How can we do that? Only through our knowledge of the Word. The Bible says that the *Word* of God is the *power* of God unto salvation—unto whatever it is you need—to those who believe (Rom. 1:16). And Jesus, the Living Word, said, "Without Me, you can do nothing" (John 15:5 *NKJV*).

You can't stand your ground against the devil in your own wisdom or strength. But you *can* successfully stand against him in the power and the authority of the Word of God. Your knowledge of the Word will enable you to take your God-given authority over all the power of the enemy (Luke 10:19). God has called you to bear much fruit (John 15:8). He has called you to enjoy the many blessings He has given. He has called you to stand your ground and have power over all the power of the enemy so that you are not destroyed or even harmed in any way, shape, form, or fashion.

Know Your Enemy

So what does the Word say about your enemy, Satan? We've looked at what the Word has to say about overflow, but it's important to realize that we have an enemy who doesn't want us to enjoy life or live above the limits he has placed on our life. So first, we must know who our enemy is. Let's establish right now that the enemy is not, and never will be, God. God is not our enemy; He's for us! He loved us enough to send Jesus Christ to die for us to secure our eternal well-being. No, our enemy is Satan, and we must understand how he operates in order to stand against him.

Even in the natural, when waging war, an army has to understand something about the enemy it's fighting in order to marshal its forces successfully. One thing we know about our enemy is that he is a master of disguise. Second Corinthians 11:14 says that he masquerades as an angel of light.

The devil likes to work stealthily, or secretly, so that we are not even aware that he is the one causing our problems. But as we look at John 10:10 in depth, we are already aware that anything that comes to our lives to steal, kill, or destroy is ultimately a work of our enemy!

Through the years in Church history, there has been much confusion and controversy over this very subject. So many tragedies and calamities have been perpetrated by Satan and then blamed on God that even some Christians' perception of God has been blurred and distorted. But John 10:10 is a foundational verse for knowing the difference between Satan's activities and God's activities. And it is clear that Satan is the thief—he's behind everything that steals, kills, and destroys—and that God is the giver of life. In fact, Jesus said He came to give us life to the full, till it overflows!

We can know with certainty today that God provided us with life more abundantly, or life till it overflows. But we should also know that if we're going to possess and enjoy that life, we must learn how to deal with our enemy, Satan. And just by reading John 10:10 as it applies to Satan, we can see that his activities consist of *stealing, killing,* and *destroying.*

It's important to realize that the devil doesn't have anything good planned for you. In fact, the devil doesn't have anything good at all! He is corrupt, and everything he has and does is corrupt. He is a thief! He doesn't have anything good to add to people's lives—he only *takes away from* people. Now, he may offer something that looks or sounds appealing, but in the end, whatever Satan has to offer will have the effect of stealing, killing, or destroying.

In the Garden of Eden, the devil didn't approach Eve, saying, "Go ahead and eat of the forbidden fruit. The moment you do, you will die spiritually. You will no longer be clothed with the glory of God. You will be separated from God's Presence. And you will plunge all of mankind into a state of sin and separation from God."

No, Genesis 3:4–6 records what the devil, the serpent, actually said to Eve.

> **GENESIS 3:4–6**
> 4 "You will not surely die," the serpent said to the woman.
> 5 "For God knows that when you eat of it your eyes will be opened, and you will be like God, knowing good and evil."
> 6 When the woman saw that the fruit of the tree was good for food and pleasing to the eye, and also desirable for gaining wisdom, she took some and ate it. She also gave some to her husband, who was with her, and he ate it.

Did the devil tell Eve the truth? No, he lied to her. He made it seem as though it would benefit her to disobey God's instructions.

The Bible talks about the pleasure of sin lasting for a season (Heb. 11:25). According to the Bible, sin provides pleasure for a season, but in the end, it brings stealing, killing, and destroying. And we already saw that Satan himself can masquerade as an angel of light. So the enemy is not going to come at you saying, "Hi, I'm the devil. I've come to steal from you and to destroy you!"

You must settle once and for all that the devil is God's enemy and your enemy! And the devil doesn't have anything good to offer at all. We know there are three basic things that the devil does: steal, kill, and destroy. He is a thief, a killer, and a destroyer. What does he want to destroy? *The things of God.*

A thief is someone who takes something that's not his. We call that *stealing.* As Christians, we belong to Christ; we don't belong to Satan, the thief. So we need to be careful about our conduct. For example, do we take copy paper, pens, and other supplies home from our workplace? Unless our boss tells us we can have those things, taking them is stealing. In thought, word, or deed, we don't want to have anything to do with the thief, Satan!

Encounter With a Thief

Our text says, *"The thief comes only to steal and kill and destroy; I have come that they may have life, and have it to the full."* Notice the first three words of that verse. Jesus said, *"The thief comes . . . ."* That means that the thief will come to *you.* Sooner or later, every one of us will have an encounter with the devil. And in every situation, I can tell you what he will try to do: steal, kill, or destroy!

I'm not telling you this to frighten you, but to prepare you. We might as well be ready for it. Jesus said that the thief comes to steal, kill, and destroy. This means that at some point in time, the thief will come to try and steal from, kill, or destroy us. There's no doubt about it.

Some people think, *Well, maybe I can avoid it somehow.* Don't waste your time or energy trying to avoid being confronted with stealing, killing, and destroying. Instead, keep feeding on the

Word of God so you'll be ready to successfully confront the devil and enforce his defeat in your life. Jesus defeated Satan and his works in His death, burial, and resurrection. But you must *stand* your ground against the enemy and enforce that defeat in Jesus' Name. If you don't, he's going to steal from you and perhaps even destroy you.

Mark 4:15 says, *"Some people are like seed along the path, where the word is sown. As soon as they hear it, Satan comes and takes away the word that was sown in them."* This verse talks about Satan coming and taking away, or stealing, something. What is he stealing? The Word—the Word that was sown in a person's heart. But I have good news for you! When the thief comes to you, you don't have to be alarmed. When he comes your way, you have what it takes to run him off!

So keep reading, studying, and meditating on the Word of God. That's what the devil is after—the Word of God that you have put in your heart. If he can steal that Word from you, he can have a heyday in your life. He can keep you from having life more abundantly and living in the overflow. He can steal what God meant for you to have.

Did you know that you can be a Christian, a child of God, and yet lose the abundance God meant for you to have? You can let the devil steal it from you (and he *will* steal it if you'll let him).

Now, I'm not saying that if you allow your blessings to be stolen, you won't go to Heaven. You'll go to Heaven, all right, but you may miss out on the things God intended for you to enjoy while you were here on earth.

One of the biggest tricks of the enemy is to convince people to think, *Well, this is just the way it has to be. I'm limited in life. I'll just have to live with lack here on earth. But someday when I get to Heaven, it will all be different. Things will be better then.*

Exercising Spiritual Authority

If you are a Christian, you are *in Christ*; and Satan has no legal rights to you—to steal from, kill, or destroy you. You are God's temple, His property, and Satan has no legal claim to that which belongs to God. But if Satan can get you to doubt God's Word and believe his lies, he can have access to you. That's why you need to exercise your spiritual authority, your God-given authority, over Satan and all his cohorts!

> **MATTHEW 28:18–19**
> **18** ". . . All authority in heaven and on earth has been given to me [Jesus].
> **19** Therefore go and make disciples of all nations . . ."

What was Jesus telling those believers to do? He said, "Go in My authority!" Jesus has attained all authority in Heaven and on earth, and He has given that authority to His Body, the Church of the Lord Jesus Christ. That means the devil and demonic forces have no authority where you are concerned unless *you* give it to them.

The Word tells us we can run Satan off when he tries to trespass on our property. To demonstrate our ability to exercise this kind of authority, I will share with you a personal illustration.

Lynette and I have two dogs, a black Labrador Retriever named Princess and a Golden Retriever named Blue. Both dogs are very territorial and they enthusiastically guard the boundaries of our property.

Recently, I heard Blue and Princess both barking ferociously, so I went outside, and I saw a stray dog on our property. Now, I obviously don't have anything against dogs. But I didn't recognize this one, and I didn't know if it was carrying some kind of disease or infestation that could affect my dogs. So I ran it off.

Now, I didn't need to ask my neighbor to come over and run that stray dog off my property. *I* did it because it was on *my* property! And that dog had no right to be there!

That stray dog would have been in trouble had it somehow gotten into the fenced area where our dogs were. Once I found a dead possum on our patio that Blue and Princess had killed. The possum had trespassed into their territory, and those dogs made that possum pay the price.

Spiritually speaking, do you want Satan trespassing into your territory—into that which belongs to you? No, you wouldn't want some kind of varmint on your property in the natural; and you certainly don't want Satan on your property—on anything that pertains to your life! But when he tries to trespass, you can make him pay the price. How? By exercising your spiritual authority and by refusing to let go of God's Word until you are enjoying every blessing and benefit He has provided for you. The devil is like a varmint—he's up to no good. So run him off with the Word and with the Name of Jesus, the Name above all names!

To Stop a Thief, You Must Stay Alert

The reason the enemy can take advantage of some people is that they are not alert spiritually. They just sort of float along through life—that is, until some crisis hits.

In First Peter chapter 5, God gave us some insight on how to avoid being blindsided by the enemy.

> **1 PETER 5:8–9**
> 8 Be self-controlled and alert. Your enemy the devil prowls around like a roaring lion looking for someone to devour.
> 9 Resist him, standing firm in the faith, because you know that your brothers throughout the world are undergoing the same kind of sufferings.

In the *King James Version,* verse 8 says, "The devil, as a roaring lion, walketh about, seeking whom he *may* devour."

We don't have to be a victim of circumstances. This verse tells me that *we*—not our circumstances—have something to do with whether or not we are devoured by the enemy. We know he has come to steal, kill, and destroy. But that doesn't mean we are destined to a life of being robbed and destroyed!

So what do we do? Well, we have to be self-controlled and alert, as verse 8 says. But we also have to put up a little fight!

> **JAMES 4:7**
> 7 Submit yourselves, then, to God. *Resist the devil, and he will flee from you.*

Some believers just roll over and play dead—like a possum—as soon as the enemy starts stirring up circumstances and imposing limitations against them. Perhaps they think, *Well, he'll flee from So-and-so, but not from me.* Or they might think, *He'll flee from Jesus, but I'm pretty helpless to do anything about my situation.*

You might feel limited and helpless in your own strength to do anything about whatever it is you may be facing. But you are not helpless *in Christ.* And in the Name of Jesus, and by His authority, you *can* resist the devil. And the devil will flee from you like he would flee from Jesus.

But notice who's doing the resisting? Is it Jesus who must resist the devil on your behalf? No, *you* are to do the resisting! And the devil will flee from *you!*

Someone said, "Yeah, but I resisted the devil, and my situation hasn't changed."

You have to stand your ground; you have to maintain your position of faith in the Word. The devil will try to wear you down until you grow weary and quit exercising your faith in God's Word.

Part of resisting the devil is resisting his lies—those thoughts, feelings, and suggestions that go against what the Word says. You have to resist fear, doubt, and unbelief—any temptation to distrust God. As you do, the enemy won't be able to wear you down or even weaken you, because you have made God and His Word your refuge and tower of strength (Ps. 18:2). (In the next chapter, we will look more in depth at the subject of persevering in faith.)

Avoid Trouble by Avoiding Sin!

Let's look at another verse that goes right along with James 4:7.

EPHESIANS 4:27
27 and do not give the devil a foothold.

The *King James Version* says, "Neither give place to the devil." Do not give the devil any place in your life! Do not give him so much as a foothold!

You know, if you don't want stray animals hanging around your house, you can't encourage them to stay. In other words, you can't give them any place by feeding them or petting them. If you do, they won't leave. Similarly, we can't give the devil any encouragement to hang around us. We have to put our foot down, so to speak, and command him to leave. Then we have to make sure we're not doing anything that would encourage him to stay.

Well, we just read Ephesians 4:27, which says we are to give the devil no place. How do you give the devil no place? First, you make up your mind, if you haven't already done so, that you and the devil are not playing on the same team.

Let me explain. It seems that some believers want to obey and serve God some of the time and then hang out with the world some of the time and act just like an unbeliever. If that describes you, you are setting yourself up to be taken advantage of by the enemy. You may think that what you're doing is all fun and games. But the devil is not playing games! He's playing for keeps! That's one reason why James said we are *to resist* him (James 4:7).

We as believers should not so much as entertain thoughts that would give the devil the idea he can hang around us. And we certainly shouldn't go places where he and his crowd are. The Apostle Paul said in First Thessalonians 5:22 that we are to abstain from all appearance of evil. Notice he didn't say, "Stay away from all evil," which we certainly should do. He said, "Stay away from all *appearance* of evil." That means that if something even looks like it could be evil, *stay away from it*!

Proverbs 4:14–15 says something similar to First Thessalonians 5:22.

PROVERBS 4:14–15
14 Do not set foot on the path of the wicked or walk in the way of evil men.
15 Avoid it, do not travel on it; turn from it and go on your way.

I can't tell you how many times I've heard Christians compromising themselves where these verses of Scripture are concerned by saying, "Well, to reach the unreached, I have to go where they go." These Christians may legitimately want to be a blessing, but they are putting themselves in harm's way. They are putting themselves in a position to be hurt.

It's fine to want to be a witness to the unsaved around you. That's what we as Christians are supposed to be—*witnesses*. But you have to draw the line at hanging around and fellowshipping with unbelievers. If you don't, their lifestyle will affect you one way or the other. I learned that as a teenager.

One time, I was riding in a car with a group of guys from school. Everything was fine until the majority of them decided to make some trouble. I spoke up immediately and said, "Guys, I'm not going to do that."

They ridiculed me, saying, "C'mon, Hagin. You're being chicken!"

At first, I responded by saying, "Well, let's take it outside, and we'll just see who's chicken!" Then I simply said, "Stop this car and let me out *now*!"

They said, "Well, you'll have to walk then."

I said, "I'd rather walk than do what you guys are about to do."

Now, I'm not trying to pin roses on myself—I'm just telling you what happened to illustrate that we have to keep ourselves out of harm's way. We can't wait for someone else to do it for us. In my case, I didn't want to be in the position I was in, so I removed myself from the situation. I shunned the appearance of evil.

The Help of the Spirit in Our Safekeeping

Another time, just after I graduated from high school, my dad called me from another state, where he was holding a meeting. He said, "Ken, get on a bus and come up here."

I questioned him, saying, "Why, Dad? I want to look for a job and try to get into college."

He said, "I was praying, and the Lord told me to tell you to get out of town right now."

I quickly agreed, packed a suitcase, got a bus ticket, and went to be with my dad.

Three days later, policemen came knocking on the door of our house. They were looking for me! My mother said, "He left on Friday. He's in another state."

"Where's his car?" they asked. Mom showed them where it was parked outside the garage just behind our house, and they explained to her their special interest in my car.

As it turned out, someone had just come through town and stolen a bunch of hubcaps. Someone caught a glimpse of the car the person was driving, and it fit the description of my car almost exactly. They asked her if anyone had used my car recently, and my mom answered no and showed them the keys.

Afterward, the policemen determined that I couldn't have committed the crime, and they left. Later, they caught the guy who had done it. He was driving a '53 Plymouth just like mine, and it was loaded with hubcaps, fender skirts, and so forth.

Now, if I hadn't left town in response to what the Holy Spirit said to my dad, I would have put myself in harm's way—just because of the car I drove!

I was 18 years old when that happened. I could have told my dad, "I'm not coming." I could have refused to leave town. But I had enough sense to know that if the Lord was saying something, I had better pay attention!

Many times, we override something down on the inside of us that's "scratching" us as if to say, *"Hey, I wouldn't do that if I were you."* And oftentimes, we think, *Oh, that was just me*, and we go on and do it anyway. When we do that, we put ourselves in a position to be attacked by the enemy. We don't take the time to pray so we can be sensitive and attuned to the Holy Spirit, Who is trying to warn us.

I'm talking about exercising spiritual authority to stay out of danger or trouble. We have an enemy, and he is out to steal, kill, and destroy. But Jesus came to give us life more abundantly—to the full, till it overflows!

The Thief Defeated

Throughout the Bible, we have record of the devil stealing, killing, and destroying. But we have no record of Jesus ever stealing, killing, or destroying. On the contrary, in the Book of Acts, Peter is recorded as saying, "How God anointed Jesus of Nazareth with the Holy Ghost and with power: who went about doing good, and healing all that were oppressed of the devil; for God was with him" (Acts 10:38 *KJV*).

In John 10:10, Jesus said, "I have come that people might have life more abundantly." When Jesus said that, He was making a proclamation. He was making an announcement: "I have come to defeat the thief. I have come to stop Satan from stealing, killing, and destroying. I have come to release humankind so that they can live above life's limitations and in the abundance I have planned for them!"

And in His death, burial, and resurrection, Jesus did just that. He defeated Satan in spiritual combat, securing our release from Satan's authority and dominion and from all that would steal, kill, or destroy.

I want you to understand that you already have the blessings of God laid up in your account because of what Jesus did at Calvary. If you've been born again, you already have the abundant life that Jesus came to give. You're not *going to* get it; you *have* it! But to enjoy it, you must stand your ground in faith, exercising your spiritual authority.

Jesus took His place as the Savior, Redeemer, and Lamb slain from the foundation of the world (Rev. 13:8) to secure life for us. He fulfilled God's plan of redemption for us. Now it's time for you and me to take our place and receive everything the Lord has done for us. We can't do it if we don't learn how to stand our ground and contend for these blessings. We must learn how to deal with the devil—how to stop a thief!

Yes, Jesus already defeated him, but if we refuse to exercise our spiritual authority over him, the thief will run roughshod over us. He will continue to steal from us and bring destruction to our lives if we don't stop him in his tracks with the Word of God and the Name of Jesus.

Most Christians don't realize they have this kind of authority. My dad used to tell of a pastor who went to visit one of his church members who was bedridden with some kind of sickness. The pastor tried to encourage the man to take authority over the enemy in his life. He even instructed the man: "Tell the devil to take his sickness and leave your body!"

The dear man replied, "I just don't feel like I'm in a position to antagonize anyone right now."

Some people think that whatever happens, good or bad, is the will of God. They think that God is in control of everything and everyone on the earth and that He is causing sickness, disease, war, poverty, and other tragedies.

These people are completely ignorant of the fact that Satan is the enemy, not God, and it is Satan who is causing all the destruction in the world. They either don't know or have forgotten that Satan gained a certain amount of control with the fall of man, when Adam and Eve disobeyed God in the Garden of Eden. Second Corinthians 4:4 calls Satan the god of this world. And until his lease runs out, he will exercise all the control and influence he possibly can to steal, kill, and destroy.

People will argue, "Well, if it's the devil who's causing all the destruction, why doesn't God do something? Why doesn't God stop him?"

God *did* do something about the devil over 2,000 years ago! He sent His Son, Jesus Christ, to destroy the works of the devil on our behalf (1 John 3:8). Now, what will we do with the Savior? What will we do with the truth of God's Word? Will we hide from the truth and shrink from acting on the Word? Or will we rise up in the power and authority of the Master Himself and destroy the works of the enemy that hinder us?

We are in error if we are waiting for God to do something about the devil. God is waiting for *us*! It's up to us as the blood-bought Church of the Lord Jesus Christ to use our God-given authority to stop the thief in our lives!

Don't Quit—Payday's Coming!

We've been looking at the will of God for us concerning God's blessings and the abundant life that Jesus came to provide (John 10:10). However, as we consider the will of God concerning those blessings, we must know not only how to receive what God has given, but how *to persevere* as an overcomer until we actually experience His blessings.

It's not enough to know that God wants to bless us. We must understand how to live in His blessings. And we must realize that these blessings are not going to fall on us like ripe cherries off a tree, as my dad used to say. In other words, just because something is the will of God doesn't mean it's automatically going to happen.

That's where we've missed it. We've thought that if something is God's will, it's just automatically going to happen, whether we get involved with it or not. But there's a giving *and* a receiving side to the blessings of God. God has given certain things to us. Now it's up to each one of us to learn how to receive, or appropriate, what He has given.

We could say that the blessings of God are ours for the taking. But we haven't understood how to take them. We haven't understood that we have to stand our ground and that we might have to stand that ground for a while. But if we'll stand full of faith and confidence in God's Word of promise to the point that we will not be denied, then we will not come up short.

Perseverance is the key. Perseverance is what it's going to take if we're going to survive—and thrive—till "payday" comes.

Any champion athlete will tell you that the goals he has reached and the honors he has attained did not come through persevering for a while and then giving up. He may use different words to describe the keys to his success, but the message will be the same. He didn't give up! He didn't quit! Whatever the opposition and whatever the odds, he persevered and continued doing the things he knew how to do. *He fought the good fight!* And in the end, he overcame and was rewarded.

Similarly, it's going to take patience and perseverance to be a champion in life. If you are going to receive from God what He has promised, you are going to have to *continue* in the faith—not just believe God one day and doubt Him the next. But if you are willing to give your all to receiving God's best, you *will* succeed!

God wants you to have life to the full, till it overflows. But this abundance does not always come right away. You have to take hold of it by faith, and when you do, you can't allow yourself to grow tired of *continuing* in faith.

Remain Faithful to God's Plan and His Promise

When Lynette and I first started out in ministry, we were believing God for financial increase and for overflow in our finances. But naturally speaking, the pickings were slim in those days. I was an associate pastor earning very little money in that position. At the end of the week, we would pay our bills, and we felt blessed if we could go to the local mall and buy a corn dog and a Coke to share. Sometimes at the end of the week, we had enough money left over to buy *two* corn dogs and a Coke!

Lynette and I would often sit there in the mall eating our corn dog, just watching the people milling around about us. Then we'd go window-shopping. As we passed certain store windows, we would talk about the fact that we knew there would come a time when we would be well blessed financially.

Thank God, that time did come. But it didn't come without some perseverance on our part. We stayed with the will of God, even when it didn't look like that particular place in the will of God was profiting us very much. We stayed faithful even in the hard places, both to the *plan* of God—to wherever He had us at that time—and to the *promises* of God, His unchanging Word.

I want to encourage you to hold on to the promises of God at all times, even when it may look as though nothing is happening. In the case of our persevering for financial blessings, there were many, many times in our lives when it looked as though our living in abundance was never going to happen.

There were many times when it looked as though things were never going to get any better for us. At one time, we lived in a tiny apartment that had been converted from a garage. That apartment had a very small kitchen and eating area, one bedroom, and one bathroom. All our living space was the equivalent of the square footage of a regular two-car garage. It was our home—but it was definitely limited!

Yet we continued to serve God and believe for the day when we would walk in God's blessings financially. There were times Lynette would sit down to pay the bills, and she would say, "Just naturally speaking, there is no way our income will match our outflow." But we kept believing and trusting God.

To this day, we don't know how we made it at times. I mean, although no extra money came in, at the end of the month after all the bills were paid, we would actually have a few dollars left over!

I'm not sharing this to get you to feel sorry for me or to complain about how bad we had it. I share it to help you see that there is victory at the end of your fighting the good fight of faith. If you will hold on to the promises of God, you will win! You'll come out victorious on the other side of whatever it is you're going through.

If you're going to have the abundant life Jesus came to give, there will be a fight that will take place. Championships do not come automatically; you have to work hard for them, and you have to endure. Similarly, the blessings of God do not come automatically.

Yes, Jesus paid the price for your victory, your deliverance, your health and soundness of mind and body, and your prosperity.

But you have an enemy who is going to throw up every smoke-screen he can in this earth realm, in the realm of your senses, to try to get you to back off from believing and trusting God. You are going to have to persevere through the pain, through the obstacles, and through the thoughts, feelings, and suggestions that come to try and tell you that God's Word is not true or that it's not true for you.

The enemy will do everything he can to keep you from receiving the abundant life and living in the overflow. But Jesus said that He came to give it; that means He wants you to have it!

You might be saying, "Yes, but what I'm living in now is nowhere close to being abundant."

You're going to have to start talking abundance and believing abundance before you ever see abundance. It doesn't matter where you're at right now. What matters is what you're believing and saying. Does what you're saying line up with God and His Word or with the limits imposed by your circumstances? What you say and continue to believe will be what you ultimately experience.

I'm not saying you should deny the circumstances and just confess that they don't exist. But I *am* saying you should look beyond the natural facts, or circumstances, to the greater facts of God's Word. God was greater than the circumstances the Israelites faced as they prepared to enter their Promised Land. And God is greater than *your* circumstances. He's greater! And if you will hold on to Him and His Word, you will enter your own promised land, the place of victory in Christ that God has provided for you.

To obtain God's blessings and live in abundance requires a fight. Don't ever think that you will just coast through life, taking it easy, and have abundance just come knocking at your door. But you will not have to fight a natural fight. You will have to fight the good fight of faith by refusing to give up on God's Word, even when the circumstances don't line up.

Your Work Will Be Rewarded

In the natural, you have to work hard to get promoted on a job. You have to persevere through some things that don't always suit you or make you happy. But people do it every day. They work hard consistently. They endure long hours. Why? Because they expect their work to be rewarded.

It seems that, spiritually, some believers can't endure even one opposing circumstance before they're ready to give up and quit! They don't have their eyes on the Word. Their focus is easily shifted from what God has said to what the circumstances are saying. They don't persevere, and they often give up right on the brink of their breakthrough! They don't persevere in faith, and they certainly don't stand their ground against the devil. They just accept as final authority every limitation that comes their way. They live a life of limitations and defeat instead of victory—a life of lack instead of overflow.

In a day of fast food, drive-throughs, convenience stores, ATMs, instant credit, and high-tech communication systems, including instant Internet access, we have become a society that wants immediate results and instant gratification. We simply don't want to wait anymore. Now, I'm not saying that the things I just listed aren't good. I'm simply saying that these things can become detrimental if we're not careful. For example, we can spend money today that we haven't even earned yet. And that can cause a problem, especially if we overspend.

Some people think that walking by faith is some kind of get-rich-quick scheme. Then when things don't change overnight, they give up and go on to something else. But let me tell you, if you will walk by faith consistently and stay faithful and obedient to God and His Word, in time, God will make you rich. I didn't say you would be a millionaire, but God will cause you to enjoy a full supply. But it doesn't happen overnight.

That's why you have to learn how to persevere in faith—because the enemy will try to keep these things from coming to pass in your life. He will try to keep you from receiving what God wants you to have. You have to fight the good fight of faith (1 Tim. 6:12), and contend for those promises.

Will You Fight or Faint?

Over the years, I have seen many people start out believing God for things, but they grew tired after a period of time and gave up on God. They were excited at first, but when the answer didn't come as soon as they thought it should, they quit believing. They fizzled out in their faith. Some even quit reading the Bible, praying, and going to church. They began living life far below the level where they should have been living.

Did you know that every minute you remain in faith about something, you are a minute closer to realizing the fulfillment of what you are believing for? But if you give up and quit, you stop your blessings in their tracks.

The Bible talks about not becoming weary in well-doing (Gal. 6:9). It also says, "In due season we shall reap, if we faint not" (*KJV*). The *New International Version* says, *"Let us not become weary in doing good, for at the proper time we will reap a harvest if we do not give up."*

You see, we need to keep on "doing good" and remaining faithful to God and His Word, because if we won't faint, or give up, payday is coming!

In the natural, on your job, you may get paid every week, every two weeks, twice a month, or once a month. Now, if you get paid once a month, for example, you wouldn't quit that job because you didn't get paid every Friday, would you?

Well, spiritually speaking, you shouldn't quit and give up on God and His Word just because you didn't see the answer when you thought you would. Remember, we *will* reap our harvest and see our answer if we don't give up!

My grandfather farmed cotton many years ago in the Blacklands of north central Texas. He would prepare the soil, plow the fields, and then plant. But after he did all that, he didn't go back two weeks later complaining, "I might as well not tend these fields. It's been two weeks, and nothing is happening."

No! There is a proper season for reaping a harvest! Maybe you've never done any farming or even planted a vegetable garden. But have you ever planted a rose bush? With many varieties of roses, when you put the bush in the ground, there aren't any roses on it. The bush consists of what looks like sticks and thorns. But before long, roses begin to bud and flower on that bush.

I want you to understand that you have to stay with some things long enough to see them produce something in your life. I've been talking about natural harvests. But when you plant the imperishable seed of the immutable, unchangeable Word of God, you can be sure that if you'll not grow weary, you *will* reap a harvest from that seed every time!

We do not have to grow tired of confessing the Word. Our continual confession of God's Word will strengthen us. As we believe the Word and continually speak it, we'll get stronger and stronger because we'll know that payday—that day when we will see and enjoy the promise—will eventually come.

Let's look at someone in the Bible who didn't grow weary in well-doing and didn't faint in his faith. Instead, the Bible says this man grew *stronger* in faith.

> **ROMANS 4:18-21**
> **18** Against all hope, Abraham in hope believed and so became the father of many nations, just as it had been said to him, "So shall your offspring be."
> **19** Without weakening in his faith, he faced the fact that his body was as good as dead—since he was about a hundred years old—and that Sarah's womb was also dead.
> **20** Yet he did not waver through unbelief regarding the promise of God, but was strengthened in his faith and gave glory to God,
> **21** being fully persuaded that God had power to do what he had promised.

I want you to notice that verse 21 says Abraham was *"fully persuaded that God had power to do what he had promised."* You have to be fully persuaded that what God has promised, He is also able to perform!

Let's look for a moment at the life of Abraham, who is called the father of faith. What was it about Abraham that caused him to be fully persuaded and caused God's promise—something that was humanly impossible—to come to pass in his life?

First, we need to understand that Abraham didn't receive his answer overnight. In fact, it was 25 years from the time Abraham was promised a son until he finally received that promised son. By the time Isaac was born, Abraham was 100 years old!

During that 25-year period, Abraham had many opportunities to give up—to grow weary and faint in his faith. Abraham didn't have the Word of God, the Bible, like you and I have it today. But he had God's promise. The Lord had said to Abraham, "Your off-spring will be as numerous as the stars in the sky and the sand on the shore" (see Gen. 22:17). So every day, Abraham saw the sand, and every night, he looked at the stars to remind him of what God had said to him.

God had told Abraham that his descendants would be innumer-able. But Abraham knew he couldn't have innumerable descen-dants until he first had one descendant! He had to believe for one before he could believe for many. Yet he and his wife Sarah were too old, naturally speaking, to have children.

Has God promised *you* something that seems impossible? Maybe you're struggling with the fact that God has provided abun-dance for you, and you're walking in lack. I want to encourage you to do as Abraham did. Just as Abraham had the stars and the sand to look at day after day, you have the Word of God—all of God's promises—to keep in your view. As you look at those promises day after day and keep them in your heart and in your mouth, you will grow strong in faith like faithful Abraham. Though the days may pass with no manifestation of what you're believing for, do not weaken. Instead, grow stronger and stronger in faith.

"Well, what does Abraham have to do with us?" someone asked.

As we know, Abraham did receive his promised son. We are to imitate the faith of people like Abraham, who persevered and received what God promised. We have the right to receive the same kinds of blessings that Abraham received. In fact, God calls those of us who have been born again Abraham's seed.

> **GALATIANS 3:29**
> **29** If you belong to Christ, then you are Abraham's seed, and heirs according to the promise.

What does that mean? It means that we can have the same kind of faith Abraham had. Abraham grew "strong in faith, giving glory to God; and being fully persuaded that, what he [God] had promised, he was able also to perform" (Rom. 4:20–21 *KJV*).

After all those years, Abraham could have weakened in his faith, but he didn't. Likewise, we can follow Abraham's faith and receive our promised blessing too!

When Faith Fizzles

Certain characteristics often accompany someone who has grown tired in his or her Christian walk, which we will look at in the following paragraphs.

First, someone who is fainting in their faith instead of fighting the good fight of faith is someone who is *forgetting to do the basics of Christian living.* He isn't reading his Bible regularly. His prayer life is faltering. Soon he runs out of spiritual fuel, and he becomes too weak to fight the faith fight.

Second, someone who is growing weary in well-doing is *forgetting his purpose.* He gets his eyes off the fulfillment of God's promise and begins to lose interest. He loses his motivation for believing God, because he has cast off his vision for seeing the Word come to pass.

Proverbs 29:18 says, "Where there is no vision, the people perish" (*KJV*). The *New International Version* says, *"The people cast off restraint."* That's why you sometimes see people who were once excited about the Word of God, yet now they're not even walking with God anymore. They forgot their purpose and their vision for the Word and the will of God for their lives. They grew weary and fizzled out with no vision or example before them.

Hebrews 6:12 says, "That ye be not slothful, but followers of them who through faith and patience inherit the promises" (*KJV*). We need to follow the faith of those who hold steady and persevere to receive the things God has promised. We are to follow their example of perseverance in receiving the blessings of God.

Third, someone who is fainting in his faith is *comparing himself to others.* This is a trap people can fall into. When they compare themselves to others, they end up trying to live up to someone else's standards. When they do, they will often find themselves falling short. But God never called you to live up to someone else's standards; He called you to live up to *His Word.* And His Word has standards you can live up to, because His commands—His words—are not burdensome or hard to follow (1 John 5:3).

You can never go wrong when you're following the Word of God. What happens, though, is we get caught focusing on where someone else is in their life, and we try to live up to them as our ultimate standard. Then discouragement sets in, and we become weary in well-doing.

You should never compare yourself to someone else. Maybe that other person is at a higher level of faith than you are at the moment. Perhaps he has developed his faith to a higher degree. Certainly, you should follow his faith and his example, as we just saw. But to compare yourself to that person is setting yourself up to fail.

I will give you a natural illustration of what I'm talking about. Suppose you go to a local gym and decide to start lifting weights. What if you were to work out with a guy who has been pumping iron for years? Would you be able to keep up with him? You're just starting out; you've never lifted weights before. So there's no way you're going to be able to lift the amount of weight that other guy is lifting. If you try to stay up with him, you might end up becoming discouraged and quitting altogether. You might even end up injured!

If you start at a beginner's level and continue lifting weights at the gym, you'll get stronger and stronger. You'll begin lifting more weight, and your muscles will get bigger or become stronger. Similarly, the more you study the Word of God and learn how to exercise and develop your faith, the stronger in faith you'll be. Your "faith muscles" will get bigger, and you'll walk in more and more of the fullness of God. It won't happen overnight, but it will happen if you persevere and keep your eyes on Jesus, not on other people.

Fourth, someone who is growing weary in well-doing is *failing to maintain a constant confession of God's Word.*

A person who doesn't maintain his confession of the Word will one day be praising God and the next day be wringing his hands, saying, "What am I going to do?"

James, under the inspiration of the Holy Spirit, had something to say about wavering, or not being constant, in your faith.

> **JAMES 1:6–8** (*KJV*)
> **6** But let him ask in faith, nothing wavering. For he that wavereth is like a wave of the sea driven with the wind and tossed.
> **7** For let not that man think that he shall receive any thing of the Lord.
> **8** A double minded man is unstable in all his ways.

James says, "If you waver in faith, you're like a wave tossed here and there." In other words, you're not constant or stable. You are up one day and down the next. People like that can't receive from God, because God requires that we walk by faith and stand our ground, unwavering.

To receive God's blessings and live above life's limits, in the overflow, we must stand strong and maintain a constant confession of God's Word, even when it looks as though things are falling apart and pressing in around us. When things look bad, God's Word remains the same! His Word is constant. Therefore, we're going to have to be constant, too, as we take our stand on the Word.

When some people hear teaching on the subject of faith, they often say, "You're teaching people to deny the circumstances."

No, we who teach Bible faith don't teach people to deny the facts. We recognize the facts, the natural circumstances that challenge us. But then we acknowledge the *greater facts* of God's Word. Armed with the greater facts, we carry on in faith, confessing the Word, not the problem.

We must not only have a positive confession of God's Word on our lips, we must maintain, or *hold fast to*, that confession of faith. We can't have lazy faith. We already read Hebrews 6:12, which says, "That ye be not slothful [or lazy], but followers of them who through faith and patience inherit the promises" (*KJV*). That word *patience* means "constancy" or "perseverance."

Now let's look at a verse that talks specifically about holding fast to your confession of faith.

> **HEBREWS 10:23** (*KJV*)
> **23** Let us hold fast the profession of our faith without wavering; (for he is faithful that promised.)

Remember, we saw that the word *patience* in Hebrews 6:12 means "constancy" or "perseverance." We must understand that it is through faith and patience—constancy or perseverance—that we receive the promises. We have to be constant, persevering in our confession of faith. We can't be hit-and-miss, or up one day and down the next.

The way to abundant life may not be instant or easy, but you can get there by faith, by continually speaking the promises of God. Continually confess that God is able to do what He has promised and then refuse to waver or back down from your confession. Keep God's Word before your eyes. Read, study, and meditate on it often. As you keep the Word in your heart and in your mouth, you will grow stronger and stronger in your faith. Adverse circumstances won't be able to keep you down. You'll be solid, steady, and stable on your faith.

Helps and Hints for Maintaining a Rock-Solid Confession

The following are four practical steps that will help you maintain your position of believing God and receiving His promise.

Number one, set aside at least five minutes a day to review the specific verses that promise you what you need or what you are believing for. Look at them. Proverbs 4:20–21 says, *"My son, pay attention to what I say; listen closely to my words. Do not let them out of your sight, keep them within your heart."*

In praying for people years ago, my dad would often spend a moment or two talking to them about what they wanted to receive from God. He would ask them, "What scriptures are you standing on?" And often, he would receive the reply, "Well, not any in particular." He would then tell them, "That's what you're going to receive then—nothing in particular!" And he would try to help them see the importance of finding scriptures that promise whatever it was they needed or wanted from God.

We know that God has provided in Christ everything we could ever need or want. Every promise in God's Word is ours to enjoy. Whether it's healing, finances, deliverance, or *whatever* you need, God's Word covers it! So find those scriptures that promise you the things you want. Then spend time looking at them every single day.

Number two is closely related to number one: Write down those promises and carry them with you wherever you go.

You could also make multiple copies and place them in various places in your home, such as on the refrigerator, on your bathroom mirror, and so forth. That way, you would be keeping them before your eyes more frequently.

Number three, make your lips do their duty! Be sure that you speak these promises over and over again. Set goals for yourself. For example, you could begin by quoting those verses three times a day, once at breakfast time, once at lunchtime, and once at dinnertime. Lynette and I do this almost constantly. Whenever we pray at mealtimes, thanking God for our food, we confess whatever promises we're standing on and thank Him that He is bringing those things to pass in our lives.

Number four, following in the steps of Abraham, be sure you are constantly giving glory to God.

> **ROMANS 4:20** (*KJV*)
> **20** He staggered not [didn't waver] at the promise of God through unbelief; but was strong in faith, giving glory to God.

If you will give glory to God constantly, praising and thanking Him for His Word, you will grow strong in faith too. You see, Abraham gave glory to God before he ever had a son. Likewise, you need to begin to give glory to God before you ever see whatever it is you are believing for. Abraham didn't wait until Isaac was born before he started giving glory to God. No, he glorified God before the promise ever came to pass!

Jesus said in John 15:5, *"Apart from me you can do nothing."* That means that apart from the Word, we can do nothing, for Jesus is the Living Word. We need to keep God's Word before us constantly, reading it, meditating on it, speaking it, and praising God for it. Don't let the Word depart from your view. Don't allow yourself to get tired of believing the promises of God. An overcomer must persevere in his or her faith.

It may look as if nothing is happening. But as you persevere in faith, I can assure you that in the unseen realm, something is taking place. If you will stand your ground without wavering, you will eventually overcome and experience the fulfillment of the promise of God in your life. So don't quit in the hard times. Payday's coming!

part three

Purposes for Living in the Overflow

chapter 9

How Your Giving Affects Your Living

With all the teaching we've received on God's will for our abundance, we need to understand that our *living* is also directly connected with our *giving*. Now, I know that when I mention giving, some people get happy, and some people get sad. And some people just want to get away from me as fast as they can!

When we think of giving, we usually think about giving of our time, our talent, and our money. We can give of almost any of the resources we have, including our salvation! For example, we could lead someone who's not saved in the sinner's prayer. We could tell someone how to be saved, how to receive Jesus as Lord and Savior and experience the New Birth for himself.

We know that living in the overflow above life's limits has to do with more than just money. Similarly, giving has to do with more than just giving money. But in this chapter, I'm going to focus predominantly on giving and on the blessings of God as they pertain to finances.

Let's examine God's Word on giving. Luke 6:38 is an important verse that encompasses many areas of giving and receiving.

> **LUKE 6:38**
> **38** Give, and it will be given to you. A good measure, pressed down, shaken together and running over, will be poured into your lap. For with the measure you use, it will be measured to you.

My dad often quoted this verse. He testified a number of times about how God used him to give into the lives of others and then how God blessed him as a result of his giving. For example, one time God told Dad to give a certain amount of money to a visiting minister who was struggling financially. It was the equivalent of a week's salary for Dad, but he gave it anyway.

Then the Lord specifically led my dad to give another significant amount to another man, and again, Dad obeyed. Two years later, God used my dad in a spectacular way to minister deliverance to someone. Afterward, the Lord spoke to him and said, "If you hadn't obeyed Me in those two instances, I never could have used you like this today."

We need to learn to hear and obey the voice of God when He speaks to us. We need to trust Him so implicitly that when He is telling us to give something, we are confident He is well able to supply our needs and bless us above and beyond what we can imagine.

Did you know that God's ability to use us is directly connected to our obedience when He tells us to do something, and that includes giving? Whether or not we obey affects our level of blessing in the future.

God may speak to you to make an investment in the life of someone else or in a particular ministry. It may look to you as though you're just going to lose money if you obey. But if you will trust God and obey Him, He can cause increase to come into your life over and above your highest expectations. God will cause blessings to come your way that wouldn't have come otherwise.

The Blessing of the Tithe

We must believe that God will pour out His blessings on those who give—on those who obey His Word concerning finances.

MALACHI 3:10–12

10 "Bring the whole tithe into the storehouse, that there may be food in my house. Test me in this," says the Lord Almighty, "and see if I will not throw open the floodgates of heaven and pour out so much blessing that you will not have room enough for it.

11 I will prevent pests from devouring your crops, and the vines in your fields will not cast their fruit," says the Lord Almighty.

12 "Then all the nations will call you blessed, for yours will be a delightful land," says the Lord Almighty.

Some people want to argue, "Well, tithing was just for those under the Law. It's not for us today, because we're not under the Law." But if you'll study the life of Abraham, you'll find that he brought tithes before the Law ever went into effect.

What is the tithe? The tithe is something that belongs to the Lord; it's 10 percent of whatever God gives us—of whatever increase comes to us. So if we get a dollar, for example, 10 cents of that belongs to God. The tithe is the first dime off every dollar we receive.

So since the tithe is something that already belongs to God, we're really not *giving* to God until we've rendered to Him our tithes. Then, after we've satisfied that obligation, anything we give above and beyond that is considered a gift.

I am so thankful that I was taught to tithe as a young boy. Every time my Paw-Paw came to visit, he would give me money. Immediately, I would run to my dad and say, "Paw-Paw gave me such-and-such amount. How much is my tithe?" Then I would separate my tithe from the rest of my money, and I would take my tithe to church on Sunday mornings and put it in the offering.

I have tithed all my life, and I'm so glad I have. What are the benefits of tithing? Let's look at Malachi 3:10–12 again to see. The first part of verse 10 says, *"Bring the whole tithe into the store-house, that there may be food in my house."*

The rest of that verse says, *"Test me in this,' says the Lord Almighty, 'and see if I will not throw open the floodgates of heaven and pour out so much blessing that you will not have room enough for it.'"*

Maximum Flow—a Flood of God's Blessings

Have you ever seen a dam? If you have, did you notice the spill-ways, or the floodgates? Have you ever been to the Hoover Dam, a great American landmark, which sits on the Colorado River? When those floodgates are opened, the water flows through very, very rapidly—several thousand cubit feet per second. The power generated by that water is about four billion kilowatt-hours or five billion horsepower per year! It is a powerful, unstoppable force!

Similarly, when we consistently obey God in our finances, He opens up floodgates and pours us out unstoppable blessings!

Some people have the attitude, *Well, I don't know whether God's going to open up the gates or not.*

He will if you believe and trust Him and persevere in faith.

Somebody said, "Well, I tithed and gave an offering last week, and I haven't seen anything yet." God never said, "I'm going to bless you by Thursday." But payday *will* come if you don't give up or quit! The blessings of God will begin to flow if you'll remain faithful to Him and His Word.

There is a dam at Keystone Lake on the Arkansas River in Oklahoma. When you're down river, you can look at the river and tell whether there's any water flowing out of that dam. When there's no water flowing out—when the floodgates are closed—the riverbed is dry. You can see little pools of water here and there, but if there's been a dry season, you can drive for long stretches on the riverbed and see nothing but sand.

But when those floodgates are opened, you had better get out of there, because you know a flood is coming!

I once heard about a man who was riding his four-wheeler in the Arkansas River with his boys. The river was dry, but suddenly they noticed a few inches of water flowing gently across the riverbed. They continued to have fun for awhile, riding through the water on their ATVs. But after a short time, the father noticed the water rising significantly higher and higher. He yelled at his sons, "Hey, they've opened up the gates! Let's get out of here!" They barely made it out of there before that riverbed was flooded with water.

Maybe you've received a measure of God's blessings already, and you're enjoying splashing around in a gentle "river" of His goodness that has come your way. But don't stop there. God wants to do more. He wants you to receive more so you can give more! The measure of the blessing you're enjoying right now is like the water flowing over that dry riverbed. It is just an indication of something greater to come—a flood of God's blessings!

God said in Malachi 3:10 that His opening the *floodgates of Heaven* is dependent on our tithing and giving. So we know that He is not withholding blessings from us. When we learn to receive from Him by faith and then bless others from the resources God has blessed us with, He opens those floodgates and sends us *a maximum, unstoppable force of blessings!*

That's powerful, isn't it? God has promised to pour out blessings from the floodgates of Heaven! But notice that God didn't stop there. Verse 11 says, *"'I will prevent pests from devouring your crops, and the vines in your fields will not cast their fruit,' says the Lord Almighty."*

The Destroyer Rebuked on Your Behalf

Malachi 3:11 is referring to crops and fields, because that was the primary way people made their living back in those days. God said that He would prevent interference to their reaping their harvest or to their being paid.

As I was growing up, my dad pastored churches down in the Blacklands of north central Texas, where the soil was rich, and cotton was the main crop of that day. There is a pest known as the boll weevil that destroys the cotton plant. Well, God said He would prevent pests from devouring and limiting our crops!

When I was a child, I remember one year in particular when there was an epidemic boll weevil infestation across Texas. It seemed everyone was talking about the boll weevils during that season. But the farmers in Dad's church didn't have any infestation that year. Why? Dad had taught them to tithe and believe God. In fact, not only did they not have boll weevils that year; they enjoyed a bumper crop!

On top of that, the price of cotton went up because the supply was low, yet the demand remained high. Those men were blessed abundantly! I believe their abundant overflow above life's limitations was directly tied to their paying tithes and giving offerings.

When you honor God and take Him at His Word, God can go to work on your behalf. He can help you on your job. He can cause promotion to come to you when no one else is getting promoted. I have even seen guys in the military get promoted long before their time came to be promoted, which is very unusual. Having been in the U.S. Army myself, I can say that it seems one of the military's slogans is, "Hurry up and wait." But God doesn't care anything about red tape; He cares about your believing and trusting Him and obeying His Word.

I want you to understand something. God is not stingy. God is a giver. He likes to give, and He especially likes to give to givers. How do I know that God is a giver? Look at what He has given to us. He gave us Jesus, the Greatest Gift ever given! John 3:16 says, *"For God so loved the world that he gave his one and only Son, that whoever believes in him shall not perish but have eternal life."* And Romans 8:32 says, *"He who did not spare his own Son, but gave him up for us all—how will he not also, along with him, graciously give us all things?"*

Since God gave us His best, Jesus Christ, why would He withhold any other blessing—any lesser blessing—from us? He wouldn't! God is a giver, but He desires that we be givers too. In fact, we are to be imitators of Him (Eph. 5:1). God wants us to live above life's limitations so we can minister to others in the area of giving.

The Cycle of Giving and Receiving

Have you ever seen someone in a restaurant and said to the waiter, "Hey, give me that person's check; I'm going to pay it"? Or have you ever shaken hands with someone and left a 20 dollar bill—or larger bill—in his hand?

It seems I am always giving my grandsons money. Just recently, I was with them, and they all came over to me, yelling, "Poppy! We need some money!"

I reached into my pocket and started doling out money to my grandsons. But on that particular day, one of them had a friend standing there with him. So I gave that young man some money too.

Somebody said, "Well, you didn't have to do that." No, I didn't have to do it. But I wanted to do it! I like to give. So I gladly gave that child some money.

God has made a way for us to have abundant living through our giving. But we must be convinced that our quality of giving affects our quality of living, or we're probably not going to give. We won't be able to have faith for a return on our giving if we're not persuaded of God's will concerning giving and receiving. So let's look at a few more verses that deal with giving and receiving.

2 CORINTHIANS 9:6
6 Remember this: Whoever sows sparingly will also reap sparingly, and whoever sows generously will also reap generously.

GALATIANS 6:7–10
7 Do not be deceived: God cannot be mocked. A man reaps what he sows.
8 The one who sows to please his sinful nature, from that nature will reap destruction; the one who sows to please the Spirit, from the Spirit will reap eternal life.
9 Let us not become weary in doing good, for at the proper time we will reap a harvest if we do not give up.
10 Therefore, as we have opportunity, let us do good to all people, especially to those who belong to the family of believers.

At times in years gone by, people have said to me, "All that tithing and giving offerings is not doing you any good." But I never let talk like that bother me, because I believe the Bible, and the Bible says that God cannot be mocked! Whatever a person sows, that's what he's going to reap. And if I'm sowing obedience—if I'm acting in obedience in tithing and giving offerings—God will see to it that His promises come to pass in my life.

When you obey God and walk in line with His Word and His way of doing things, He will make His promises good in your life too. Why? Because God is utterly faithful. He is not a man that He could ever tell a lie. And God cannot be mocked. If you obey Him, He *will* bless you.

Some people mock biblical prosperity by saying, "That sowing and reaping stuff doesn't work. Those preachers are just trying to get your money."

I'm not saying that there's never been a preacher who has missed it in the area of finances, because some have missed it and have overemphasized money as it relates to ministry. But let me tell you something. Without money, a church can't keep the lights on! It takes money to pay pastors and other staff. It takes money to operate a ministry that supports missions and funds other outreaches that are getting the Gospel message out, not only to the local community, but to the four corners of the world.

In the natural, or in the secular world, how do you think a company keeps its doors open? By the finances that come in to that company! In much the same way, that's how a ministry keeps its doors open—by the finances that come in to that ministry.

Some people complain when the pastor mentions tithes and offerings. They don't tithe, and if they give, they don't give very generously. They either don't have any understanding of the Word of God concerning prosperity, or they just don't believe it. God wants us blessed. But He wants us to be blessed His way, and one of the main ways He blesses us is through the avenue of our giving.

Other people will gripe as they're tithing or giving. They're not doing it in faith, and as a result, they don't receive any blessings from their giving. The Bible says that God loves a *cheerful* giver (2 Cor. 9:7), not a giver who gives begrudgingly or unwillingly.

Giving to Live and Living to Give!

There is a cycle of giving and receiving we must get involved in if we're going to tap into God's overflow blessings and live above life's limits. We need to give to live—to enjoy the overflow—and we need to adopt the attitude that we live to give.

The Bible says that it is more blessed to give than to receive (Acts 20:35). Let me ask you a question: Would you rather be the person who has enough food to eat and can give food away so that others can eat, or you would rather be the person who doesn't have any food? One reason it's more blessed to give is that if you're giving, that means you have something to start with that you can give!

I am always amazed at those who complain about their lack of blessings and their inability to give anything away. Yet they have plenty of food to eat. They have clothes to wear, and they have a place to live. They may not have everything they want, and they may not be able to give like they really want to give, but they can give *something*. And their giving will be the vehicle by which God increases them materially and financially.

Friend, no matter where we are in life, God wants to bring us to a higher level. But it's time for us to stop complaining and start giving! I encourage you to read the Scriptures for yourself. Meditate on those verses that talk about giving. Meditate on those that promise a return on your giving when you do it with a right heart and a right attitude. Then begin to act on those promises. When you act on the Word of God in faith and trust, you will be blessed in your doing (James 1:25)!

Give Willingly and Be Faithful

As I said before, Lynette and I weren't always where we are financially today. We once lived in a wooden house with cracks in the walls so big that even with the windows closed, when the wind was blowing, our curtains would blow around like they were in an open breeze! But early in our marriage, we adopted an attitude of giving; and we were determined to obey God in this area of giving and receiving. No matter how small the amount we were able to give at the time, we gave it willingly, and we gave it in faith, trusting God. And God has never failed us yet! And He will never fail us, ever! Hallelujah!

In that old wooden house, we had one floor furnace in the living room that provided the only heat for the whole house—the living room, two bedrooms, a kitchen, and a small dining area. (The one bathroom had a small wall heater that kept that room warm.) Let me tell you—it was cold in that house in the wintertime! We would crank that furnace up as high as it would go and then turn the oven on in the kitchen to generate a little more heat. It was still ice-cold in the bedrooms. At night, we used four or five quilts to try and stay warm. After you got into bed at night in the winter, you didn't want to get back out.

On cold mornings, we had trouble getting our old car started. The motor hardly had any compression at all, and the valves were all burnt. That was in 1967. We didn't have it as easy then as we have it now. But we stayed faithful in our giving, and we didn't complain.

Today, we're able to give a lot more than we could back then, but we started giving when we were barely getting by—when life's limitations were pressing in upon us. We didn't decide to wait to give until we became more prosperous. If we had decided to wait, we wouldn't be enjoying the prosperity we enjoy today.

When Lynette was pregnant with our first child, Craig, we didn't have any insurance. I was a full-time associate pastor. And by "full-time," I mean I was on call 24 hours a day, 365 days a year! I made $50 per week. We had to trust God to help us pay the hospital bill when it came time for Craig to be born. Naturally speaking, we should have stopped giving and started saving every penny we could toward that hospital bill. Even then, we couldn't see any way to accomplish it. But we kept giving, and we believed God would make a way.

There was a man in our church who was a general contractor for a company that was building a new addition in the city. One day, he said to me, "I know you've been mowing yards and doing odd jobs trying to get money for the baby."

He continued, "Our company has made a deal with the city of Dallas, and they are allowing us to put up advertisements for this addition, but our signs have to be put out after midnight on Fridays and picked up before five o'clock in the morning on Mondays. We have a route mapped out where we want the signs and are looking for somebody to do it for us for twenty-five dollars a week. Would you be interested in the job?"

I said, "Are you kidding? I'll take it!" I put up signs and took them down every weekend for several months, sometimes in the cold and rain. But it didn't matter to me. When I checked Lynette out of that hospital in July 1969, I wrote a check for the full amount of that bill. I was able to pay the bill right on the spot! I could do it because God made a way for me to do it. He opened a door for me and gave me that opportunity because we had been obedient to Him.

Set Goals for Your Giving

Earlier, I referred to Second Corinthians 9:6, which says, *"Whoever sows sparingly will also reap sparingly, and whoever sows generously will also reap generously."*

Let's look at that verse in its context.

2 CORINTHIANS 9:6–8
6 Remember this: Whoever sows sparingly will also reap sparingly, and whoever sows generously will also reap generously.
7 Each man should give what he has decided in his heart to give, not reluctantly or under compulsion, for God loves a cheerful giver.
8 And God is able to make all grace abound to you, so that in all things at all times, having all that you need, you will abound in every good work.

Now look at verse 7, which says, in effect, "Each person should give what he has decided in his heart to do." The rest of that verse says, ". . . *not reluctantly or under compulsion, for God loves a cheerful giver.*" According to this verse, the amount you give is something that you decide in your heart to do. God doesn't want you to give begrudgingly; He wants you to give *cheerfully.*

Many times, you hear ministers say, "Ask God to show you what to give" or, "Listen to what God is saying to your heart." Certainly, there are times when God will talk to you about your giving. But when He doesn't, that's no indication that you shouldn't give! At those times, you simply need to decide in your own heart what you should give.

I'm talking about choice. God wants us to give willingly— because we choose to give—and then He gives us guidelines for choosing: "If you sow, or give, a little, you're going to reap a little. But if you sow a lot, you're going to reap a lot."

As I said, sometimes God will speak to you about what to give. And sometimes, the amount He'll tell you to give will seem to you to be a sacrificial amount. But if you will obey Him in your giving, He will bring you to another level in your living! Then at other times, God allows you to make your own decision about what to give. But your decision concerning your giving is still going to affect your living.

Previously, I talked about living large by thinking large. In other words, you have to think, believe, and speak in line with God's Word in order to enjoy the blessings that His Word promises. You can't think small—in fear, doubt, and unbelief—and live life in abundance, in the overflow. You have to think large in order to live large.

Similarly, you have to give large to live large too! Some people are trying to live large while giving little. But that doesn't work in God's system. In God's system, your giving—not your withholding—affects your living (see Prov. 11:24–25).

Usually, at the beginning of a new year, most families set certain goals. Maybe they schedule their vacation time or schedule a certain number of recreational activities for the year. Perhaps they plan things they're going to buy that year, such as large appliances or automobiles.

Goal setting is important both in the natural and in the spiritual. I believe that since our giving affects our living, we should set goals for our giving too.

Just recently I talked to someone who told me, "I have been paying tithes faithfully for years. But this year, my goal is to tithe 10 percent and then give 10 percent on top of that."

Someone else I know did something similar. He began setting goals for giving over and above his tithe, and today he is up to giving 20 percent above his tithe. That's 30 percent of his income! He said, "Every time I set a goal and meet it, the Lord gives me more income. So I just keep setting new goals."

This man's heart is in his giving. He gives because He loves God, not just to get something. He knows he's going to be blessed in his giving, but he truly desires to be a blessing and to further the work of God. He is giving and living above life's limits. His main motive for giving is to bless God.

God wants us to give because we believe and trust Him and because we want to see His Kingdom expanded. He doesn't want us giving just to see if we can get more. We are to give in faith, believing that He will bless our giving.

A Winning Game Plan

If you know anything about sports, you know that a coach develops a game plan for his or her team to execute in hopes of winning a game against the opposition. In the corporate world, executives often develop a plan or strategy for reaching certain goals for their company. They set goals and then lay out an action plan for accomplishing those goals. Spiritually, when we set goals of what we want to give to God in terms of our time, our talents, and our money, we are developing a winning game plan for our lives.

I think it is very important for us as Christians to sit down with our family and set certain financial goals each year. Decide how much you want to give for the year. Then form a plan for reaching those goals. For example, if you're married, have your spouse pray and agree with you about reaching those goals. If you have children who are old enough to understand these things, have them pray with you too. And understand this: the purpose of setting goals is not just to gain money. The purpose is to stretch and exercise your faith for something specific that honors God.

'Freely You Have Received, Freely Give'

We must realize that God has not given us the blessings we enjoy today for us to be selfish with those blessings and hoard them just for ourselves. Everything we enjoy in life—our knowledge of God's Word, the Holy Spirit, healing, and material blessings—was intended for us not only to enjoy, but to share. The abundant life, the overflow, that Jesus came to give was given so that we could have that life and then share it by giving to others and showing them that they can receive from God too. This is truly living the abundant life of overflow above life's limits.

Perhaps you've been set free in a certain area of your life, such as from deep poverty and lack. Even if you're not yet where you want to be, you need to share the power of God that you have received and help others be freed from the bondage and tyranny of the thief, Satan. Matthew 10:8 says, *"Freely you have received, freely give."* We can't lose for winning—we can't go under for going over—when we're giving of those things that we have received from God, because the more we give, the more we will receive! Our giving will positively affect every area of our life and cause us to live in the overflow, above life's limits!

About the Cover

Rev. Kenneth Hagin Jr. stands near the top of Victoria Falls, located on the border of Zimbabwe and Zambia, Africa, in March 2006. Photo by Phil Anglin.

About the Author

Rev. Kenneth Hagin Jr., President of Kenneth Hagin Ministries and pastor of RHEMA Bible Church, ministers around the world. Known for calling the Body of Christ to steadfast faith, he seizes every ministry opportunity to impart an attitude of "I cannot be defeated, and I will not quit."

Rev. Hagin Jr. began preparing for his call to ministry—a ministry that now spans almost 50 years—at Southwestern Assemblies of God University. He graduated from Oral Roberts University in Tulsa, Oklahoma, and holds an honorary Doctor of Divinity degree from Faith Theological Seminary in Tampa, Florida.

In his early years of ministry, Rev. Hagin Jr. was an associate pastor and traveling evangelist. Later, he went on to organize and develop RHEMA Bible Training Centers in Broken Arrow, Oklahoma, and in 13 countries around the world.

Rev. Hagin Jr.'s array of responsibilities also includes International Director of RHEMA Ministerial Association International. With his wife, Rev. Lynette Hagin, he co-hosts *Rhema for Today*, a weekday radio program broadcast throughout the United States, and *RHEMA Praise,* a weekly television broadcast.

Recognizing the lateness of the hour before the second coming of the Lord Jesus Christ, Rev. Hagin Jr. has expanded his speaking schedule beyond his regular pastoral duties. To fulfill the urgent call of God to prepare the Church for a deeper experience of His Presence, Rev. Hagin Jr. delivers messages that reveal key spiritual truths about faith, healing, and other vital subjects. He often ministers with a strong healing anointing, and his ministry helps lead believers into a greater experience of the Glory of God!

Rev. Hagin Jr. and his wife live in Tulsa, Oklahoma. He is the son of the late Kenneth E. Hagin.